PEGASUS ENCYCLOPEDIA LIBRARY

Experiments and Activities
BIOLOGY

Edited by: Aparna Chatterji
Managing editor: Tapasi De
Designed by: Vijesh Chahal and Anil Kumar
Illustrated by: Suman S. Roy, Tanoy Choudhury
Colouring done by: Vinay Kumar, Sonu, Kiran Kumari & Pradeep Kumar

CONTENTS

Introduction 3
How strong is an egg? 4
Which leaf preserves water? 5
Do plants drink water? 6
Making eyeglasses with fingers 8
Zigzag roots 9
The frightened earthworm 10
Self-watering flowers 11
Are you moving? 12
Do plants release water? 13
Are you stronger than air? 15
Measuring force 16
Which is quicker, gravity or the eye? 17
Lifting a water cup with the palm 18
Finding your blind spot 19
Potatoes with bird feathers 20
The lazy eye 21
Growing bread mould 22
Water with microscopic creatures 23
Flowers without stems 24
Floating lemon 25
Taste and smell go together 26
Sunlight and plants 27
How yeast breathes 28
Make your own greenhouse 29
Cells of an onion 30
How much air can your lungs hold? 31
Index 32

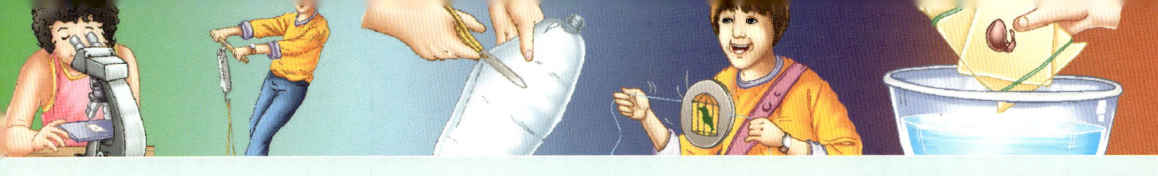

Introduction

Learning and experiencing new things is a continuous process. Children are much more inquisitive than we elders are. They are always bubbling with enthusiasm when it comes to knowing new things. That is the reason they are so full of questions. This enthusiasm should never be curbed; instead, it should be encouraged!

It is a proven fact that children learn the most by doing, experiencing and seeing things. Teaching them through books and worksheets only, does not suffice. We all know that 'seeing is believing'.

But sometimes due to the constraint of time and many other factors, elders are not successful in giving those experiences and exposure to their children which they deserve.

As a subject, Biology is important because it is the 'study of life'. It is the branch of science that tells us about plants, animals and human beings. This encyclopedia on Biology is full of interesting activities and experiments that will help the young readers to enhance their knowledge about the living things around them!

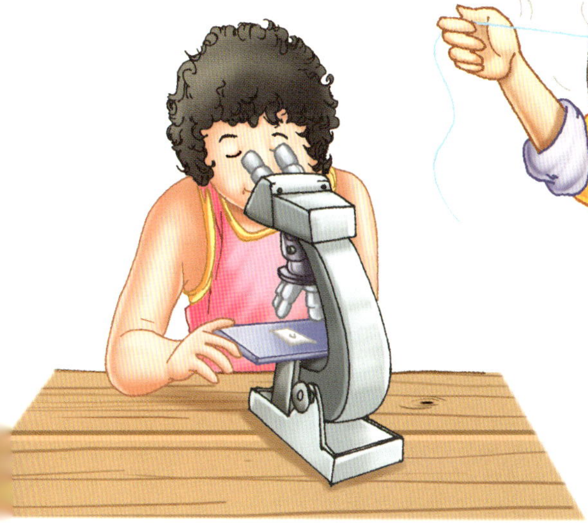

How strong is an egg?

The fact

We know that an egg is not hard to break because its shell isn't very strong. But an egg is perhaps not that fragile as it remains intact when it hits the ground when the hen lays it. Nature has taken care that an egg is both light and strong. Perform this experiment to check this out.

What you need

- A large tray
- An egg
- Clay
- A pile of coins
- A plastic bag
- Books

How to do the experiment?

1. Set the egg upright with the help of some clay on one side of the tray.
2. Put two piles of coins equaling the height of the egg on two opposite corners of the tray.
3. Place one book in the plastic bag in order to protect it and then balance it carefully on the egg and the coins.
4. Watch the egg carefully and place books on it, one by one. See how many can it hold before it breaks?

Conclusion

An egg is shaped like an arch at both ends. This is an excellent shape for bearing loads. Its strength along its axis is great because high arches spread loads. An egg is much easier to break on its sides because at the shallower arches they are weaker.

Which leaf preserves water?

The fact

Summers are often very dry. Leaves of many plants have certain structures or shapes which help them conserve moisture. Look for those which are able to retain water for the longest time.

What you need

- Cotton thread
- Different kinds of leaves
- Two tall sticks

How to do the experiment?

1. In a warm area, affix the two sticks on the ground leaving a little distance between them.
2. Tie the cotton thread between the two sticks.
3. Tie the leaves onto the thread.
4. Check the leaves every hour and note the changes observed.

Conclusion

Some leaves become very dry but some surprisingly do not look that dry. This means that these leaves have the capacity to hold back the moisture more than the others. These leaves usually have a waxy cuticle to prevent water loss. Some leaves also have curled up shapes which reduce the surface area to volume ratio, thereby decreasing water loss due to transpiration.

Do plants drink water?

The fact

We all know that water reaches plants from the soil through the roots and moves up through the stem. This experiment will show you how.

How to do the experiment?

1. Trim 1 cm off the bottom of your carnation stem and place it in the coloured water.
2. Keep it there for a few hours.

What will happen?

After sometime, the flowers will show traces of the colour of the water.

What you need

- White flowers (eg. Carnations or roses) with long stems
- Water coloured with ink or food dye
- A knife

Conclusion

The stalk of flowers contains tiny tubes called capillaries. When immersed in water, the molecules of the capillary walls which are in contact with water attract the water molecules which are the closest to them and raise them above the level of the water in the vessel. To this capillary phenomenon is added the osmotic pressure which takes the water all the way to the top of the flower.

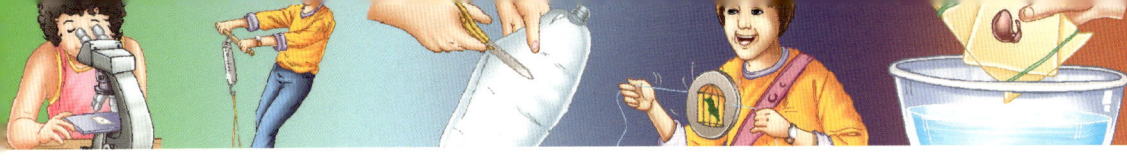

Do plants drink water?

A step further

You may also do this experiment using various food colours and see which gives the best results.

The previous experiment can be taken a step further. Read the experiment given below and see how.

What you need

- A white flower (carnation, rose, dahlia)
- Two glasses of water
- Blue and red coloured dyes

How to do the experiment?

1. Colour the water in the two glasses— one red and one blue. To get brightly coloured flowers, add more colour to the water.
2. Ask an adult to carefully slit the stalk of the flower from the middle and lower the two halves into the two glasses standing side by side.
3. Wait for a few hours.

What will happen?

One half of the flower will have traces of blue and the other half traces of the red colour!

Conclusion

The stem or the stalk of the flower contains tiny tubes or capillaries called xylem, which carry the coloured water from the two glasses to the flower. Since the two halves of the stalk are placed in different coloured water, the flower gets coloured in different hues.

Making eyeglasses with fingers

Here is an activity that can only be performed by people those who are short-sighted.

How to perform the activity?

1. Bend your index finger and thumb to form a small opening as shown.
2. Look through the hole. Distant objects will appear sharper.

What happens?

The air in the hole acts as a convex lens which corrects short sightedness by directing the image towards the central yellow spot in your eye called the macula.

> **Yellow spot** or **macula** is an oval spot near the centre of the retina of the human eye. It has a size of 1.5 mm and it is specialized for seeing things with the highest clarity.

Zigzag roots

The fact

We know that the roots of plants always grow vertically downwards. Through this experiment let's turn some soil with seeds planted in it in different directions and see if we can 'confuse' the seeds!

What you need

- Germinated seeds (seedlings)
- Two sheets of blotting paper
- Two pieces of glass
- Two rubber bands
- A shallow vessel with some water

How to do the experiment?

1. Take the shoots and place them between the two sheets of blotting paper.
2. Place the blotting paper with the seedlings between the pieces of glass and seal them with the rubber bands as shown.
3. Place the glass in the vessel with water and put it near a window.
4. Every other day, flip the glass over to the opposite edge.

What will happen?

The roots will always grow downwards while the shoot will grow upwards, irrespective of the orientation of the glass.

Conclusion

Plants 'know' the direction of the Earth's core. The Earth's gravity always makes roots grow downwards. This phenomenon is called geotropism. The plant's shoot grows in the opposite direction. If you look at plants growing on hillsides, you will see that they always grow vertically.

The frightened earthworm

Here is a harmless activity involving an earthworm.

What you need

- A copper plate and a zinc plate (both rectangle shaped)
- A strip of sandpaper
- Some water

How to do the activity?

1. Clean the plates with sandpaper and wet them with water.
2. Place them on top of each other forming a cross and put the worm on one.

What will happen?

When the worm tries to cross over from one plate to the other, it is driven back.

Conclusion

When the copper and the zinc plates are brought in contact with water, certain chemical reactions take place across their surfaces. As a result of these reactions, when the earthworm touches both the metal plates at the same time, a weak current flows through its body and it is unable to proceed ahead.

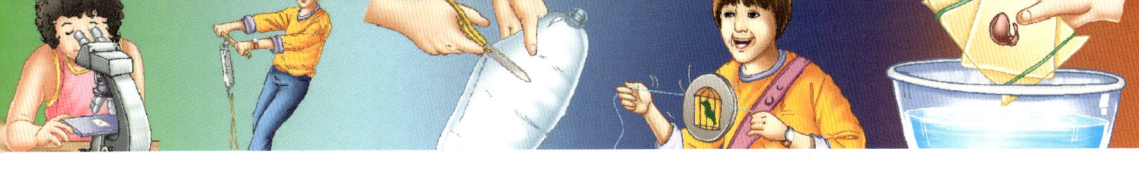

Self-watering flowers

The fact

According to the principles of hydrodynamics, a liquid will flow from a container kept at a higher elevation to a lower elevation, if connected with a tube. This is due to a difference in the potential energy of the liquids kept at different elevations. This principle can be used to water your flower pots when you are away!

What you need

- A vessel to keep water
- A base for it (e.g. a box or a high carton)
- A thin rubber or plastic tube
- A flower pot

How to do the experiment?

1. Fill the vessel with water and place it on the base. This will increase the elevation of the water vessel with respect to the flower pot kept on the floor.
2. Dip one end of the thin tube into the water vessel and put the other into the flower pot.

What will happen?

The flower pot will always have a sufficient supply of water due to the principle of siphon.

Note: When you want the watering to begin, draw the air out from the end of the tube which is going into the flower pot. The water will begin to flow towards the pot, though at a slow rate because of the reduced atmospheric pressure acting on the end implanted into the earth. Another factor which causes the siphon to work is the difference in potential of the liquids kept at the different elevations. The difference in potential is caused due to gravity.

Conclusion

Both pressure and gravity play a part in the flow of fluids. The difference in pressure at each end pushes the water into the tube. Gravity pulls the fluid downward. If the effect of the pressure works with gravity, the fluid will flow. If it works against gravity, the fluid may not flow.

Are you moving?

The fact

When we are unable to see our surroundings, it is difficult to observe the change in our position relative to other things. So, it is difficult to understand whether we are moving or not. This experiment will help you understand this phenomenon.

What will happen?

The blindfolded person will never know whether she/he is moving or not!

What you need

A blindfold

How to perform the activity?

1. One of you should be blindfolded.
2. Then two others should carry that person as shown.
3. The children who are the bearers should alternate forward steps with stepping up and down while standing still.

Conclusion

When we are unable to see our surroundings, we cannot observe the change in our position relative to other things. We will therefore not be sure if we are moving or not.

Do plants release water?

The fact

Plants absorb water from the soil. Some of this water is released into the atmosphere as water vapour by the process called transpiration.

How to do the experiment?

1. Cover the plant with the plastic bag.
2. Using the tape, seal the bag around the stem taking care not to damage the plant.
3. Wait for a day.

What you need?

- A potted plant
- Plastic bag
- Adhesive tape

What will happen?

You will observe tiny droplets on the inner surface of the bag.

Conclusion

Plants release some water through tiny pores in their leaves called stomata.

BIOLOGY

A step further

You may do another experiment in a totally different manner having the same outcome.

What you need

A large plastic jar with a wide opening

Some nutrient rich humus

Charcoal and gravel

Small plants like ivy

Ferns and mosses

About 250 mm of water

How to do the experiment?

1. Spread the gravel at the bottom of the jar. Place a layer of charcoal on top of it.
2. Put a layer of soil about 10 cm thick on the charcoal.
3. Carefully take selected plants from their pots and plant them in the jar.
4. Water the soil but make sure it isn't too wet.
5. Put the lid on the jar and place it in a warm and well-lit spot, but not in direct sunlight.

What will happen?

Tiny droplets of water will be seen on the walls of the jar.

Conclusion

Plants do give out some water out of what they have consumed.

Are you stronger than air?

The fact

Although, we are generally quite unaware of its existence, air pressure affects us all the time. Let us see this through this simple activity.

What you need

Two bathroom rubber suction cups

How to do the experiment?

1. Hold the cups together as shown and force some air out of them.
2. After sometime, try and pull them apart. You will see that it isn't as easy as it appears.

Conclusion

Placing the cups together forms a sphere. When you expel some of the air inside them, you actually help in reducing the pressure inside. The outside air pressure is then enough to hold them together tightly.

Measuring force

The fact

Force is defined as an influence that tends to cause an object to undergo a change in speed, direction or shape. We cannot see force itself, but we can see its effect. In order to move an object from a state of rest or to be stopped, a force must be exerted on it.

All people exert force by using the strength of their muscles. If you have a dynamometer or a spring scale, you can measure your own muscle strength in the following way.

What you need

- A spring scale
- A bottle and a cork stopper
- A corkscrew
- A piece of cord

Note: The dynamometer works on the principle of an elastic spring – the stronger the force, the more the spring is extended and further it moves the pointer.

How to do the activity?

1. Loop one end of the cord around your foot and attach the other to the dynamometer.
2. Pull the dynamometer upwards.

What will happen?

The pointer on the dynamometer will move and show the force which you are exerting.

A step further

You can also measure the force needed to extract a cork from a bottle, with the use of the dynamometer.

Which is quicker, gravity or the eye?

The fact

Gravity is a mysterious force. Everyone knows that it exists yet it is very difficult to understand it. It is gravity that is responsible for the planet Earth attracting all other objects. When you see images of astronauts seemingly floating in space in a state of complete weightlessness that does not mean that the Earth is not exerting a gravitational force on them. Here is a way to use the force of gravity for a game.

What you need

- White cardboard
- A ruler
- A pen and a pair of scissors

How to perform the activity?

1. Cut out a piece of white cardboard 30 cm long and 5 cm wide.
2. Mark 5 cm divisions on the cardboard making six segments in all.
3. Ask a friend to hold the cardboard hanging vertically just above your hand.
4. When your friend drops the cardboard, try and catch it as quickly as you can.
5. What will happen?
6. However easy it looks, you will never be able to catch the bottom end of the cardboard.

A step further

Have your friend drop a ping pong ball down a tube held vertically. Try and smack the ball with a ruler as it leaves the tube and before it hits the ground.

Conclusion

This happens because it is a race between gravity and your body. By the time the message from your brain reaches the muscles of your hand, gravity pulls the cardboard down several centimetres.

17

BIOLOGY

Lifting a water cup with the palm

What you need

A plastic cup full of water

How to perform the activity?

1. Place the cup full of water on the table.

2. Moisten the palm of your hand and press it down flat on the cup, bending your fingers as shown.

3. Now straighten your fingers, but continue to press down on the cup.

4. Now lift your hand slowly.

What will happen?

The cup will stay attached to the palm of your hand.

Conclusion

By pressing down on the cup you expel a little air. This makes the outside air pressure stronger than that of the rarified air inside and that it what holds the cup attached to your hand.

Finding your blind spot

What you need

A piece of cardboard inscribed as shown below with a cross and a dot.

How to do the activity?

1. Hold the strip exactly 38 cm from your eyes, close your left eye and focus the other eye on the 'X' written on the cardboard.
2. Slowly move the strip closer until first the square and then the dot disappears.
3. Keep moving the strip closer until the square and the dot appear again.

The fact

The blind spot in the eye does not contain light-sensitive cells and does not respond to light. So the images that fall on it are not seen at all.

What will happen?

When the image of the square falls on the blind spot it won't be seen. The same happens with the black spct.

Conclusion

The Blind Spot does not contain light-sensitive cells and does not respond to light. In other words, it cannot transform light into nerve impulses as it happens in the Yellow Spot (the sensitive region of the eye's retina).

Potatoes with bird feathers

The fact

This experiment will show the effect of bird feathers as they fly through the air.

What you need

- A small potato
- Six to eight bird feathers

How to do the experiment?

1. Drop the potato and note its flight through the air.
2. Now stick the feathers into the potato as shown in the picture and drop it from the same height.

What will happen?

The potato drops more slowly and rotates as it falls.

The feathers provide strong air resistance, while the featherless potato has an easier time forcing its way through the air.

A step further

Try and run with an open umbrella trailing behind you and then run without it. Which will be easier and why?

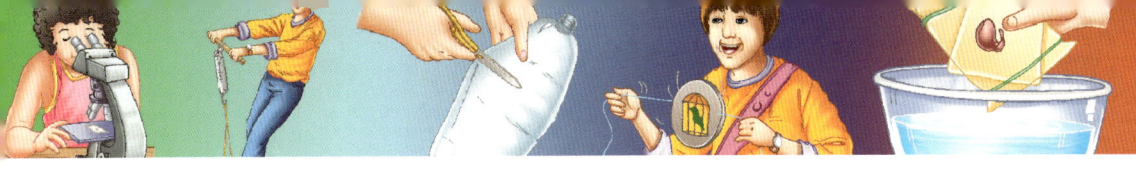

The lazy eye

The fact

Our eye retains an image for a fraction of a second after it has disappeared. This is due to the 'laziness' of the eye.

What you need

- A piece of cardboard
- A pin
- Two pieces of string and a pencil

How to do the activity?

Cut out a circular piece of cardboard.

1. On one side draw an empty cage and on the other a bird (upside down).
2. Make two small holes with the pin on both the sides of the circular cardboard. Insert strings through them and fasten.
3. Rotate the strings a number of times and then pull them apart rotating the cardboard.

What will happen?

It will appear as if the bird is inside the cage!

Conclusion

What happens is the effect caused by the 'laziness' of the eye. This means that our eye retains an image for a fraction of a second even after it has disappeared. When the image of the cage appears, the image of the bird still lingers in our vision. The two images merge with each other forming a single image of a bird in a cage.

Growing bread mould

The fact

Perform this experiment to demonstrate that Bread Mold spores are present anywhere and everywhere.

What is a Bread Mold?

Bread Mold is a simple fungus which gets its food from a variety of materials like grains, fruits, vegetables or flesh. Mold spores are tiny and usually remain suspended in the air. As soon as it finds the right environment for it to grow, the spores transform into the living fungus.

What you need

- Piece of bread
- Re-sealable airtight plastic bag
- Dropper
- Cotton swab
- Milk carton
- Adhesive tape
- Water
- Disposable rubber hand gloves for protection

How to do the experiment?

1. Collect dust from the ground on a piece of cotton cloth.
2. Rub this soiled cloth on a slice of bread.
3. Put 5 or 6 drops of water on the bread slice.
4. Put this bread slice in an airtight bag and seal it.
5. Place this sealed bag in an empty milk carton (preferably with milk remains in it) and seal the carton.
6. Leave the set-up undisturbed for a day or two.

What will happen?

After two days, when the sealed package will be opened, the bread slice will be covered with Bread Mold of various colours and textures.

Conclusion

Spores develop into living fungus when it gets suitable conditions. The bread slice had adequate nutrition and moisture necessary for the Mold spores to germinate.

Water with microscopic creatures

The fact

Water is generally the home to many interesting creatures and microorganisms, especially if its dirty water. Take some samples, view them under a microscope and see what you can find.

What you need

- A concave slide
- A dropper
- A microscope
- Different samples of water (tap water, pond water, muddy water etc).

How to do the experiment?

1. Set up your microscope using its highest setting.
2. Use the dropper to take some water from one of your samples and put it on the concave slide. Focus the microscope properly and try to see the living organisms swimming in it.
3. After observing their movements you can record their behaviours and draw them too.

What are you looking at?

Some of the creatures and microorganisms you might be able to see include:

Euglenas: Any unicellular organism belonging to the genus Euglena that lives in freshwater, have a cylindrical or sausage-like shape and move by means of a whip-like flagellum.

Protozoa: Any of a large group of unicellular, usually microscopic, eukaryotic organisms, such as amoebas, ciliates, flagellates and sporozoans.

Amoebas: Amoebas are one-celled protozoa. These microorganisms swim by wobbling. They also surround their food like a blob in order to eat it.

Algae: These are not considered to be plants by most scientists; these organisms might be yellowish, greenish or reddish in colour.

There might be larger creatures such as worms or brine shrimp in your water samples depending on where you took them from.

Flowers without stems

The fact

We know that stems are a necessary part of a plant for its survival. This activity will help you understand this.

What do you need

- 2 fresh flowers
- Scissors
- Pencil or pen
- Journal

How to do the activity?

1. Cut the stem of one of the flowers using a pair of scissors.
2. Place both the flowers (one with the stem, one without a stem) in a safe place.
3. After an hour, check the plants and note any noticeable difference in your journal.
4. Now wait for 24 hours and check the plants again. Do not forget to take down the differences in your journal.
5. Repeat step 4 for 2 more days. Observe what happens to the plants.

What will happen?

The flower without the stem will wilt off much faster than the flower with the stem.

Conclusion

The stem of a flower holds water whether they are in a vase or in the ground. The stem draws up water to keep their petals moist and healthy. When the stem was cut off from one of the flowers, its water source was naturally cut-off also. So, the flower wilted. And on the other hand, the flower that had the stem remained fresh for a much longer period of time.

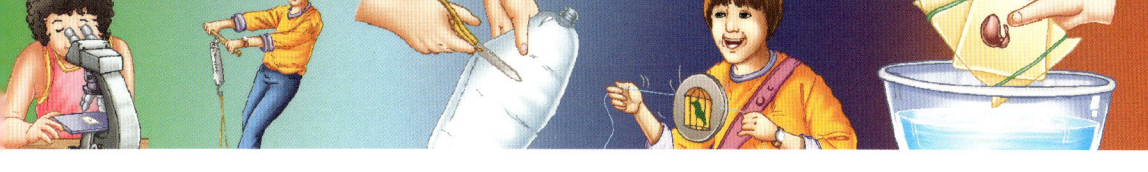

Floating lemon

The fact

To determine whether a lemon will float in water or sink to the bottom.

What you need

- Whole lemon
- Bowl
- Water
- Knife
- Cutting board

How to do the experiment?

1. Fill the bowl with water in such a manner so that its about 3/4 full.
2. Place the whole lemon into the water. It floats!
3. Now cut the lemon into 4 pieces.
4. Place all the lemon pieces individually into the water. What happens?

What will happen?

The lemon sinks once it has been cut into 4 pieces.

A step further

You could try this experiment with other fruits as well. Can you think of a fruit that would always sink, regardless of being cut or not?

Conclusion

When the lemon pieces are put into the water they sink! This is because the lemon pulp gets filled with water after being cut. The weight of the water causes the lemon pieces to sink to the bottom of the bowl. The outer skin of the lemon is waterproof. And so, when not cut, due to this waterproof skin the lemon doesn't sink.

Taste and smell go together

The fact

We all know that some foods taste better than others. But have you ever thought what gives us the ability to experience all these unique flavours and tastes? This simple experiment shows that there's a lot more to taste than you might have thought before.

What you need

- A small piece of peeled potato
- A small piece of peeled apple

Note: both the fruits should be of the same shape so that you won't be able to tell the difference.

How to do the activity?

1. Close your eyes and mix up the pieces of potato and apple.
2. Hold your nose and eat each piece. What will happen? Can you tell the difference between the two fruits?

What will happen?

It will be difficult to tell the difference between the two fruits as you were holding your nose.

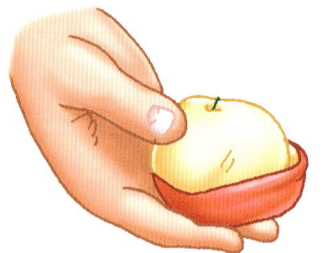

Conclusion

Our nose and mouth are connected through the same airway which means that you taste and smell foods at the same time. Your sense of taste can recognize salty, sweet, bitter and sour food; but when you combine this with your sense of smell you can recognize many other individual tastes as well.

Sunlight and plants

The fact

We all know that plants need sunlight in order to survive. This experiment will prove this.

What you need

- 2 plastic cups
- 2 saucers
- 2 seedlings
- soil
- water
- scissors

How to do the experiment?

1. Make some small holes in the bottom of the cups. This will help in draining out extra water from the cups.
2. Fill each cup with soil.
3. Plant a seedling in each cup in the centre of the soil and then cover it with soil again.
4. Place each cup on a saucer and pour equal amounts of water in both the cups.
5. Place one plant in a brightly lit room where it will get plenty of natural sunlight such as on a window sill.
6. Place the other plant in a dark area, devoid of natural light. Such locations include closets and drawers where doors can be shut and light kept out.
7. Leave both plants undisturbed for 3 or more days.
8. After several days have passed, observe your plants.

What will happen?

The plant that was placed in the dark room with no sunlight becomes limp and unhealthy, possibly even dead after only a few days. On the other hand, the plant which was kept in the sunlight, survived well.

Conclusion

Plants need natural sunlight to survive. They can be happy, healthy and growing only if they get the adequate amount of sunlight. This is because sunlight helps the plants to produce food, allowing them to stay healthy.

BIOLOGY

How yeast breathes

The fact

Most microorganisms are harmful to human beings as they cause various diseases. But some can also be very useful. We use them to make yoghurt, cheese, bread and beer. Yeast is a microscopic fungus which when dried looks like a yellowish powder. When observed under the microscope, it is found to consist of live cells. The given experiment shows how the yeast breathes.

How to do the experiment?

1. Put a teaspoonful of sugar and a small quantity of yeast into the bottle.
2. Add a little warm water. Shake to mix the ingredients.
3. Fix a balloon firmly over the neck of the bottle.
4. Pour warm water into the large vessel and put the bottle into it.

What will happen?

The balloon will blow up after sometime.

What you need

- A bottle
- Some sugar
- Dried yeast
- A large water vessel
- A balloon

Conclusion

After you have poured the warm water onto the yeast, it 'wakes up' and begins feeding on the sugar. As it does, it releases carbon dioxide during respiration and blows up the balloon with that gas.

Make your own greenhouse

What are we doing?

Creating a miniature greenhouse to grow living plants.

What is a greenhouse?

Greenhouses are structures made with glass or plastic and are mostly used to grow vegetables, fruits, plants, flowers and tobacco. Greenhouses protect plants from extreme cold along with storms and harsh weather. They also protect the plants from damaging pests.

What you need

- A clear plastic bottle (such as a large empty soda bottle)
- Planting soil
- Small plant or seedling
- Wide tape
- Scissors
- Water

How to do the activity?

1. Wash the bottle thoroughly so that it is clean. It is okay even if its still a little wet inside.
2. Cut the bottle into half.
3. Take the bottom part of the bottle and fill it half with soil.
4. Plant the seedling or small plant in the soil making sure to cover all its roots.
5. Place the top half of the bottle back onto the bottom half and seal them together with the tape. Make sure its air tight.
6. Put a few drops of water into the bottle. Replace the cap.
7. Place your mini greenhouse near a window where it will get plenty of sunlight. Leave it there for several days.
8. After a few days you will notice that the bottle has droplets of water. If the bottle becomes too moist, open the cap and let it dry for a while.

What happened?

The sun caused the temperature inside the greenhouse to rise. As the lid was sealed the air inside got heated, even when the air outside the greenhouse was cool. Moreover, the plant inside gave out water vapour as all plants do. The water vapour came in contact with the cool surface of the bottle and condensed to form tiny droplets of water.

Cells of an onion

The fact

An onion is made of many concentric layers. Each layer is separated by a thin membrane. In this experiment, we will make a slide and look at the cells of the membrane under a microscope.

What you need

- A small piece of onion
- Forceps or tweezers
- A clean glass slide
- Dye (iodine or methylene blue)
- Thin glass coverslip
- An optical microscope

How to do the experiment?

1. Take a small piece of onion and using forceps (tweezers) peel off the membrane from beneath.

2. Lay the membrane flat on the surface of a clean glass slide then add 1 drop of dye (iodine or methylene blue).

3. Lower a thin glass cover slip over the slide. Make sure there are no air bubbles.

4. Put the slide under the microscope. Make sure that the lens is set on low power, and the light of the microscope is turned on.

5. Look through the lens carefully until you see the cells. They will look like lizard skin.

6. Now use the high powered lens so that you can see the cells magnified. You should be able to make out the nucleus too.

How much air can your lungs hold?

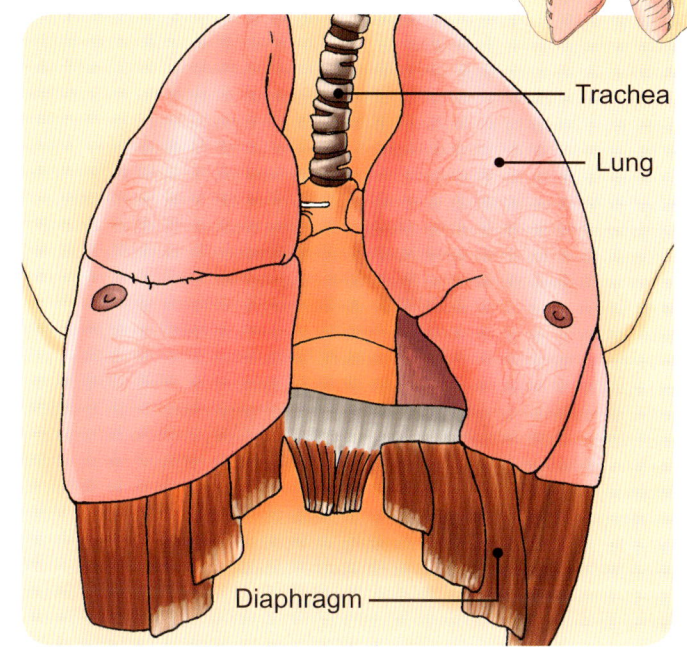

Trachea
Lung
Diaphragm

The fact

Do you think you're fit and healthy? Let's check how much air your lungs can hold.

What you need

- Clean plastic tube
- A large plastic bottle
- Water
- Kitchen sink or large water basin

How to do the experiment?

1. Clean the plastic tube.
2. Put about 10 cm of water into your kitchen sink.
3. Fill the plastic bottle right to the top with water.
4. Put your hand over the top of the bottle to stop water from escaping when you turn it upside down.
5. Turn the bottle upside down. Place the top of the bottle under the water into the sink before removing your hand.
6. Push one end of the plastic tube into the bottle.
7. Take a big breath in.
8. Breathe out as much air as you can through the tube.

What will happen?

As you breathe out through the tube, the air from your lungs take the place of the water in the bottle. If you took a big breath in and breathed out fully then the volume of water you pushed out will be equivalent to how much air your lungs can hold.

31

Index

A

amoebas 23
arches 4

B

blind spot 19

C

capillary 6
concave 23
cuticle 5

D

dynamometer 16

E

Euglenas 23
eukaryotic 23

F

fungus 22, 28

G

geotropism 9
germinate 22

H

humus 14
hydrodynamics 11

M

macula 8

magnified 30
methylene blue 30
microorganisms 23

N

nucleus 30

O

osmotic pressure 6

P

potential energy 11
pressure 6, 11, 15, 18
Protozoa 23

R

resistance 20

S

stomata 13

T

transpiration 5, 13

U

unicellular 23

Y

Yellow Spot 8, 19

PEGASUS ENCYCLOPEDIA LIBRARY

Experiments and Activities
CHEMISTRY

Edited by: Aparna Chatterji
Managing editor: Tapasi De
Designed by: Vijesh Chahal and Anil Kumar
Illustrated by: Suman S. Roy, Tanoy Choudhury
Colouring done by: Vinay Kumar, Sonu, Kiran Kumari & Pradeep Kumar

CHEMISTRY

CONTENTS

Introduction 3
Wind dries things 4
Does it float or does it sink? 5
Liquid sandwich 6
Why is it easier to swim in salt water? 7
Boat powered by liquid soap 8
Sugar and soap move objects 9
Ice needs space 10
An ice which sinks 11
Indicators 12
Which ice is harder? 14
The properties of objects 15
Making stalactites at home 16
Plastic milk 17
Metal which swims on water 18
Which is lighter, alcohol or water? 19
A cloud in a bottle 20
The magic matchsticks 21
Changes in objects 22
The shooting cork 23
Making soap bubbles 24
A salt garden 25
Restoring the lustre of aluminum 26
Burning metal 27
Fire needs oxygen to burn 28
Heat and margarine 29
Salt melts ice 30
Soap vs Detergent 31
Index 32

Introduction

Learning and experiencing new things is a continuous process. Children are much more inquisitive than we elders are. They are always bubbling with enthusiasm when it comes to knowing new things. That is the reason they are so full of questions. This enthusiasm should never be curbed; instead, it should be encouraged!

It is a proven fact that children learn the most by doing, experiencing and seeing things. Teaching them through books and worksheets only, does not suffice. We all know that 'seeing is believing'.

But sometimes due to the constraint of time and many other factors, elders are not successful in giving those experiences and exposure to their children which they deserve.

This encyclopedia on Chemistry which is termed as a 'natural science' will help the young readers to know more about the composition, structure and properties of matter as well as the changes it undergoes. They will also come to know about the chemical changes that take place in our everyday life like the combustion of fuel in our vehicles and common things like the melting of ice.

In other words, this encyclopedia will make the readers aware of the chemical changes that are going around in our lives and make them more comfortable with their surroundings.

CHEMISTRY

Wind dries things

The fact

The sun and the wind help wet things to dry which we will show in the following experiment.

What you need

Cotton cloth pieces approximately 50 by 50 cm and clothes-pegs.

How to do the experiment?

1. Soak all the cloth pieces in water, but don't wring them.
2. Hang them on clothes-lines in various spots—some in the shade where there's no wind, in the shade where its windy, in the sun where there's no wind and in the sun where its windy. You can also hang some to dry inside the house as well. Spread them out well.

What will happen?

The clothes hung in the windless and shady spots will take the longest to dry. Again, the one in the sunny and the windy spots will dry out the fastest. Stretching out the clothes properly also reduces the drying time.

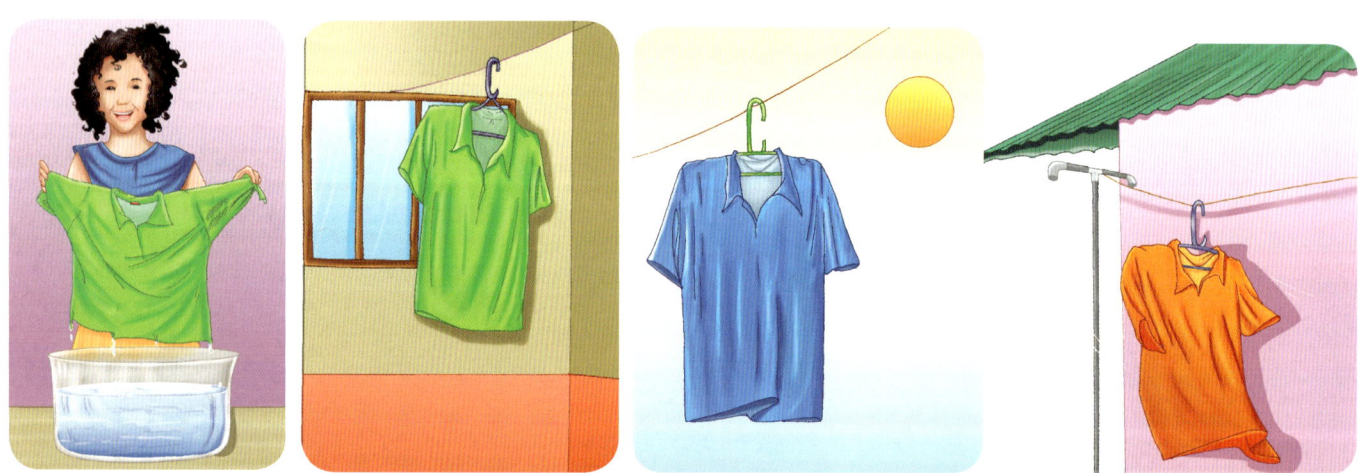

Conclusion

The sun helps in the evaporation of water. Wind is also important in this process, because it helps to carry water molecules away from the surface of the cloth.

Does it float or does it sink?

The fact

Wood, Styrofoam and ice float on water regardless of their shape and size. But materials like plastic putty or metals may either float or sink depending on their shape, which we shall show in the following experiment.

What you need

- A lump of plasticine
- Four glass marbles
- A vessel full of water

How to do the experiment?

1. Put the marbles in the water and they will sink at once.
2. The same will happen with the plasticine lump.
3. Now take the marbles and the plasticine out of the water. Form a round, shallow pan out of the plasticine. Lower the plasticine pan into the water.

What will happen?

The plasticine will float.

A step further

Measure out several equal chunks of plastic putty. Organise plasticine boat sailing competition of who can make a boat which will take the biggest number of marbles without sinking?

Conclusion

For something to float, the amount of water that it displaces should weigh more than the object. The lump of plasticine sinks because of its shape which has low surface area. The amount of water that it displaces is very less. Thus, its own weight is more than the weight of the water that it displaces. This causes it to sink. But once you shape it into a boat, its surface area increases. This increases the amount of water that it displaces. Thus, the weight of the water that it displaces is more than its weight. Hence, the boat of plasticine floats.

Liquid sandwich

The fact

Many liquids are similar to water and can be mixed with it easily. But there are also those which are very difficult to mix with water. One of them is oil.

What you need

- Water (coloured with some ink)
- Oil
- Glycerine
- A bottle with a stopper

How to do the experiment?

1. Pour equal quantities of oil and water into the bottle.
2. Close well and shake vigorously.

What will happen?

The liquids will appear to mix, but not for long. Soon the oil will be floating on top of the water.

A step further

Try adding another liquid to water. Pour in the densest liquid first, for example glycerine and then water.

Conclusion

Oil and water refuse to mix because their chemical natures vary. Oil is made of long hydrocarbons which are nonpolar. Water on the other hand is a polar molecule. Hence, oil does not mix in water. It is lighter than water; so it floats on top of water.

Why is it easier to swim in salt water?

The fact

We know that denser or heavier the liquid, the better things can float on top of it. Have you heard of the Dead Sea? Its density is the result of a very high content of salt. In the Dead Sea, you don't need to keep swimming to keep yourself on the surface. The following experiment will show you that it is easier to float in a denser liquid.

What you need

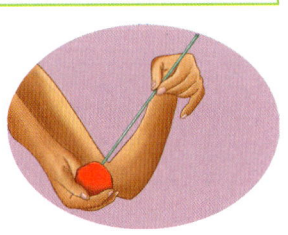

- A drinking straw
- Plasticine
- Container with ordinary water

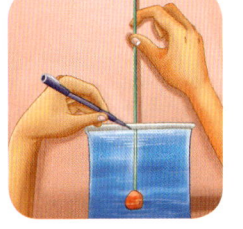

- Container with salty water

How to do the experiment?

1. Fix a plasticine ball at one end of a drinking straw.
2. Lower the straw into a vessel with ordinary water until it floats upright.
3. Mark the water level on the straw.
4. Now do the same in a vessel filled with salty water.

What will happen?

The straw will sink deeper in fresh water.

A step further

Pour some more salt into the vessel full of water and repeat the experiment. Do you see any change?

Conclusion

The particles in a denser liquid are bigger or closer to one another than those of less dense liquids. Denser liquids exert more pressure on the objects on their surface. In the case of the Dead Sea, the very salty (very dense also) water exerts pressure on swimmers preventing them from sinking.

CHEMISTRY

Boat powered by liquid soap

The fact

Oil when mixed with water weakens surface tension

What you need

- A clean tub filled with water
- Greased paper
- Some liquid soap
- A ruler
- Scissors
- A pencil

How to do the experiment?

1. Draw an equal-sided triangle on the paper with a base of about 4 to 5 cm and a height of 8 to 9 cm.
2. Cut out the triangle and place it on the surface of the water.
3. Put a drop of liquid soap on your fingertip.
4. Immerse the fingertip into the water behind the triangle's base.

What will happen?

The paper boat will move.

  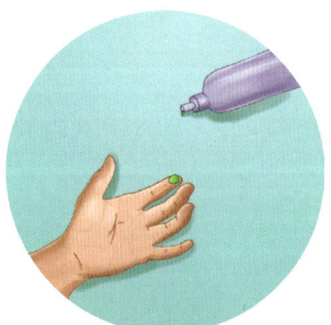 

Conclusion

The force between molecules on the surface of the water is bigger than that inside the vessel, forming surface tension. The surface of the water acts as a tight membrane. As the soap dissolves, it emits oil residues into the water. These residues weaken the surface tension and push the boat away from the spot where your finger touches the water.

Sugar and soap move objects

The fact

Soap can 'force' objects to move on the surface of water. Sugar can do the same, but the movement is different. Let's check.

What you need

- A bowl of water
- Matchsticks
- A sugar cube and a piece of soap

How to do the experiment?

1. Break the matchsticks into smaller pieces and allow them to float on the water.
2. Put the sugar cube into the centre of the bowl.
3. Now put the piece of soap into the centre of the bowl.

What will happen?

The sugar will move the pieces of wood towards the centre. And the soap will move the pieces away from the centre.

Conclusion

Sugar is porous and draws water into itself, pulling the pieces of wood along in the current it creates.

The soap, on the other hand, dissolves in water and decreases the surface tension. This propels the pieces away from the centre of the bowl.

CHEMISTRY

Ice needs space

The fact

We know that when water is cooled sufficiently, it turns into a solid form called ice. When that happens, it occupies more space than it had taken when in a liquid state. Let's prove this.

What you need

- Water
- Aluminium foil
- A funnel
- A freezer
- A small glass bottle

How to do the experiment?

1. Using the funnel, fill the bottle with water completely.
2. Place a piece of foil on the top and put the bottle into the freezer.
3. Take out the bottle out of the freezer after several hours.

What will happen?

The ice will lift the foil, showing that the water has expanded as it froze.

Note: Be careful, as the bottle may crack during the experiment.

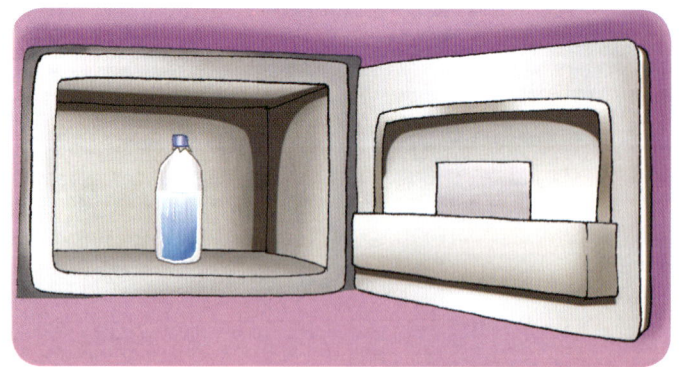

Conclusion

Most liquids get denser as they freeze, but in case of water, it is the opposite. When it turns into ice, it gets less dense and takes up more space. Ice floats on water because water is denser than ice. Icebergs float on the oceans for the same reason.

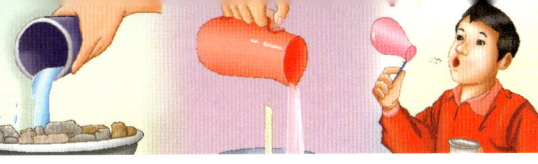

An ice which sinks

The fact

Many a time ice can sink in water even if only for a short while.

What you need

- An ice tray
- A freezer
- Water colours
- A plastic glass

How to do the experiment?

1. Pour some water into the plastic glass and mix some water colour in it.
2. Pour the coloured water into the ice tray and place it in the freezer. Let it freeze.
3. Pour some hot water into the plastic glass.
4. Put a cube of the coloured ice into the glass.

What will happen?

The cube will melt and the colour will spread through the hot water. The cube will also sink to the bottom of the glass, but after sometime it will once again rise to the surface.

Conclusion

As the ice cube melts, it turns into water. This melted ice is cooler than the warm water. Hence, it is denser. As a result, this freshly melted ice sinks. As it sinks, it is warmed by hot water and hence rises up again.

11

CHEMISTRY

Indicators

The fact

A surprising thing happens when you place pieces of red cabbage leaves in water. When you squish the pieces and water together, the water turns blue! If you add small amounts of different liquids, the cabbage-water will turn a variety of beautiful colours—pink, purple, teal or green. Try this activity to see some amazing colour changes.

What you need

- Red cabbage leaf
- Warm water
- Measuring spoons
- Measuring cups
- Plastic zip-closing bag
- 2 eye droppers
- 5 small cups (paper or plastic)
- Vinegar-teaspoon
- Laundry detergent-1 tablespoon
- 1 flat toothpick
- Masking tape
- Ball point pen

How to do the experiment?

1. First prepare the indicator solution.
2. Place the red cabbage leaf pieces into the zipped plastic bag. Add ¾ cup of warm water and close the bag tightly.

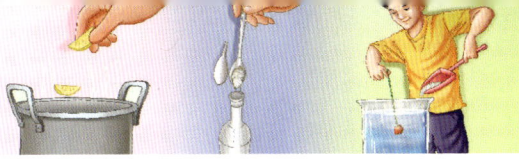

Indicators

3. Squeeze the bag of cabbage for a while and the water will turn dark blue. This dark blue liquid is your indicator solution.

Now you can begin your activity

- Using masking tape and pen, label the 5 cups as shown.
- Pour about 2 tablespoons of vinegar into the vinegar cup.
- Pour 2 tablespoons of water into the detergent solution cup. Add 1 teaspoon of detergent and swirl to mix.
- Pour 2 tablespoons of indicator solution into the three indicator cups.
- Use your dropper to put 1 drop of vinegar in the indicator + vinegar cup. Gently swirl the cup to mix. What do you observe?
- Use the second dropper to add 1 drop of detergent solution to the indicator + detergent cup. Gently swirl to mix. What do you observe?

Conclusion

Red cabbage-water is a special substance called an indicator. This means that when the colour of the cabbage-water changes, it says something about the liquid that was added to it. When the indicator is blue, it's considered to be neutral. Adding a neutral liquid like water will keep the indicator blue. You can make the indicator change to pink by adding an acid like vinegar, lemon juice or cream of tartar. The indicator will change to green by adding a base like laundry detergent or soap. Try adding different substance to red cabbage indicator and use the colour changes to classify each substance.

CHEMISTRY

Which ice is harder?

The fact

Sawdust makes ice harder. We will show this in the following experiment.

What you need

- Two round plastic containers (old butter or margarine cups)
- Sawdust
- Water

How to do the experiment?

1. Pour a little water into both cups.
2. Put some sawdust into one of them and make sure the water levels in both are equal.
3. Let both the cups freeze well in a freezer.
4. Now try to break the two ice disks.

What will happen?

The ice with the sawdust will be harder to break.

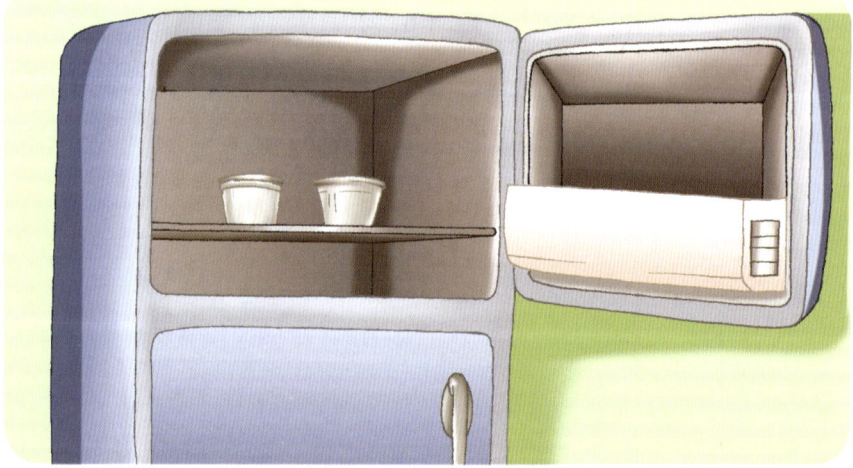

Conclusion

The sawdust acts as a reinforcement which makes the ice tougher.

The properties of objects

The fact

Every object has certain specified properties—hardness, colour, taste, smell, density, volume, inertia etc. Some of these properties change on their own, while we are able to alter others. It is easy to change the properties of cardboard and ice. The following experiments will show how.

fold the cardboard into an accordion shape; that is, make step folds in the cardboard.

What will happen?

In the latter case, the cardboard will hold up the glass.

What you need

- Three identical glass tumblers
- A piece of thin cardboard

How to do the experiment?

1. Place the two glasses apart and place the cardboard across them.
2. Place the third glass in the middle of the cardboard.
3. Now repeat the experiment, but first

Conclusion

When the cardboard is folded, many more particles (molecules) participate in holding up the glass.

CHEMISTRY

Making stalactites at home

The fact

Rainwater dissolves some types of rocks. Sometimes water seeping into a cave leaves a solid residue behind as it flows. With time, this residue forms a stalactite, a pillar hanging from the cave's ceiling. Try and make a small stalactite which will look much like the original.

How to do the experiment?

1. Make a saturated mixture of Epson salts in a vessel with hot water.
2. Cool and fill the jars with the mixture.
3. Hang the paper clips from the ends of the pieces of yarn.
4. Let the clips hang into the water-salt solution in the two jars stretching the yarn between them.
5. Place the jars in a warm and safe spot and put the saucer underneath the yarn.

What you need

- Two small glass jars
- Water
- Epsom salts
- Two paper clips
- Wool yarn
- A saucer

What will happen?

Over the following days, a stalactite will slowly grow from the yarn between the jars!

Note: Instead of Epson salts you can also use alum or sugar

Conclusion

The saturated solution soaks the yarn and slowly spreads through it. Some of it drips from the yarn. As it does, the water evaporates and leaves behind a salty residue.

16

Plastic milk

The fact

Some materials can be changed into different forms (other than their original) in which they remain. We call them 'plastic' materials. Wet clay, for example, is a plastic material, because it will retain any shape you give it. In this experiment, you will see that milk can also be transformed into a plastic material.

3. Keep stirring. In a few seconds, the milk coagulates and becomes somewhat like rubber floating on water.

4. Let this cool. Then wash the coagulated milk with cold water and examine the 'plastic' material you have produced.

What will happen?

Vinegar is an acid. When added to hot milk, it causes a chemical reaction re-ordering the milk particles.

What you need

- A saucepan
- Milk
- Vinegar

How to do the experiment?

1. Heat some milk in the saucepan.
2. When it begins to boil, slowly stir in a little vinegar.

Conclusion

The milk separates into a liquid and a solid plastic like lump. This solid is made of fat, minerals and a protein called casein.

CHEMISTRY

Metal which swims on water

The fact

Surface tension of water counteracts with the force of gravity and prevents metals from sinking in water. Due to surface tension, the surface of water acts like a stretched membrane.

What you need

- A vessel with water
- blotting paper
- a razor blade
- a metal paper clip
- a needle
- a fork

How to do the experiment?

1. Put the paper clip on a piece of blotting paper and place the paper on a fork.
2. Slowly lower the paper onto the surface of the water.

What will happen?

The paper will soon soak up water and sink but the paper clip will float.

A step further

You can do the same with a razor, a blade and a needle, and the result will be the same.

Conclusion

Metal is heavier than water and should sink. But the surface tension of the water is enough to counteract the force of gravity pulling down on the metal object preventing it from sinking.

Which is lighter, alcohol or water?

The fact

Alcohol is lighter than water. We can check this without weighing the two liquids through the experiment given below.

What you need

- Two identical small glasses
- An ordinary postcard
- Some water and some brandy

How to do the experiment?

1. Fill both glasses to the brim, one with brandy and the other with water.
2. Put the postcard on top of the water, lift the glass and turn it upside-down.
3. Place the water glass on the brandy glass and pull the postcard towards you a bit.

What will happen?

After a few minutes, the brandy will flow up into the upper glass and the water will sink to replace it.

Conclusion

Alcohol is lighter than water. When the liquids flow in the opposite directions, there is a little mixing too.

19

CHEMISTRY

A cloud in a bottle

The fact

When water is heated it turns into vapour. This vapour cools and condenses when it meets cooler air or a cooler object turning into tiny droplets of water which forms the cloud.

What will happen?

Clouds will appear in the bottle!

What you need

- A wide-necked glass bottle
- A piece of cardboard with a wide hole
- A few icecubes
- Warm water

How to do the experiment?

1. Pour some warm water into the bottle.
2. Place the cardboard over the top with the icecubes on it.

Conclusion

Water vapour which rises from the warm water, reaches the ice and is condensed as a cloud. The same happens in nature.

Water vapour rises to the cool upper atmosphere and forms clouds. Window panes are fogged in a similar manner when warm and moist air comes in contact with cold glass.

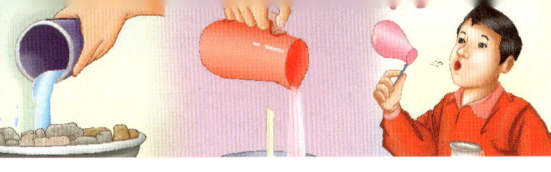

The magic matchsticks

The fact

Liquids have a tendency to rise in narrow tubes or are drawn into small openings. It is a result of the intermolecular attraction within the liquid and the solid materials. This tendency is known as Capillary action. The experiments given below will prove just this.

What you need

- A bottle
- A candle
- A cork stopper
- A pin
- A box of matches
- Water

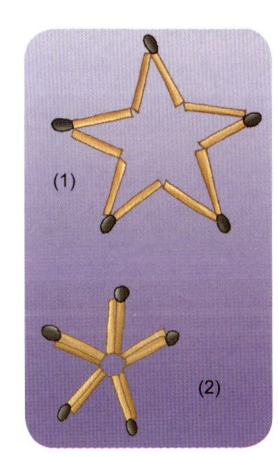

How to do the experiment?

1. Bend a matchstick so that the two halves form a right angle.
2. Pin it to the cork as shown.
3. Bring a burning candle near the match.
4. Pour some drops of water on the bended part of the match.

What will happen?

The match will straighten and burst into flame.

A step further

- Bend matchsticks into half. Place them on a plate as shown in picture 1. Drip some water on the bends. After sometime you will get a new arrangement, as shown in Picture 2.

Conclusion

The matchstick soaks up the water in tiny capillaries which causes it to straighten and come in contact with the flame.

CHEMISTRY

Changes in objects

The fact

Many a time relatively small changes done to objects can cause them to change their behaviour and assume new properties.

What you need

- A wide-necked bottle
- A hard-boiled egg
- A piece of paper
- A match box

How to do the experiment?

1. Shell the egg.
2. Put the paper into the bottle.
3. Throw in a burning match to set the paper on fire.
4. When the flames are the highest, close the opening with the boiled egg.
5. Wait for the fire to go out and the air in the bottle to cool.

What will happen?

The egg will slowly slide down into the bottle and then suddenly pop in with a bang.

A step further

You may use a banana skin instead of the egg.

Conclusion

The egg is driven down by the atmospheric pressure, which is greater outside than the thin air inside the bottle.

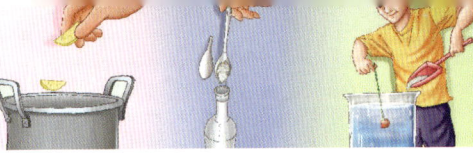

The shooting cork

The fact

Sodium Bicarbonate (baking soda) is a base which reacts with the acetic acid in the vinegar to produce water and Sodium Acetate. In the process, it also gives out carbon dioxide as a product. In this experiment we will show this.

What you need

- A bottle with a cork stopper
- Vinegar
- Bicarbonate of soda
- A table spoon
- Water

How to do the experiment?

1. Pour two tablespoonfuls of bicarbonate of soda into the bottle.
2. Wet the cork with water.
3. Pour two tablespoonfuls of vinegar into the bottle and plug it quickly with the cork (not too firmly).

What will happen?

The mixture will begin to hiss and bubble and very soon the cork will shoot out of the bottle.

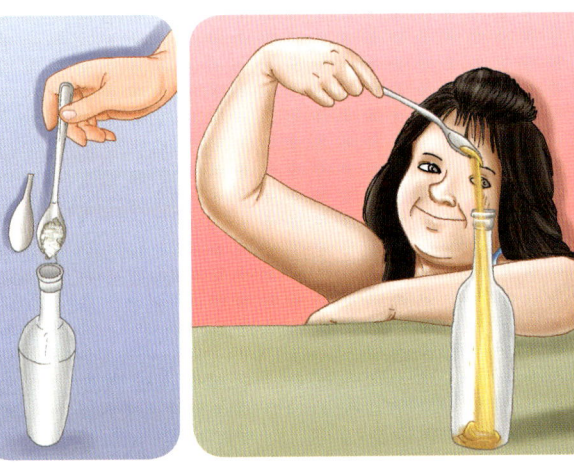

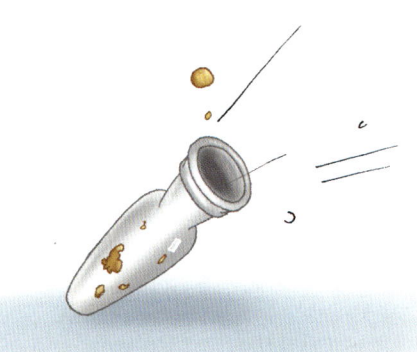

Conclusion

The cork will be expelled by the pressure of the carbon-dioxide formed in the reaction.

CHEMISTRY

Making soap bubbles

We all have been fascinated by bubbles made from soap water in our childhood. Let us make this soap solution and see whether we can still make soap bubbles or not.

What you need

- Water
- Detergent soap
- Glycerine
- A suitable vessel
- A grater
- A piece of linen

How to do the experiment?

1. Grate some soap in a container.
2. Dissolve it in warm water (the solution should be as thick as possible).
3. Strain the solution through the cloth.
4. Mix this solution with glycerine (three parts solution and two parts glycerine).
5. Let it stand for a while and then remove the white coating that will form on the surface.

How to use the solution?

Make loops out of wire, dip them in the liquid and blow bubbles in the air.

Conclusion

When you blow into the mixture of water and soap, you add the air that forms the centre of the bubble. Bubbles burst when they dry out. Adding glycerine slows down the evaporation of water that causes the drying out. Hence, glycerine increases the life of the bubble.

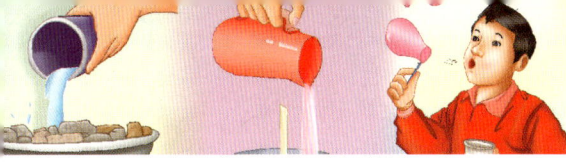

A salt garden

The fact

Liquids have a tendency to rise in narrow tubes and are drawn into small openings. It is the result of the intermolecular attraction within the liquid and the solid materials. This tendency is known as Capillary action. The experiment given below will prove just this.

- Several porous rocks or pieces of coal

How to do the experiment?

1. Put the stones on the plate.
2. Dissolve the salt in warm water to the maximum possible density.
3. Add a tablespoonful of vinegar to the solution.
4. Pour the solution over the stones.

What will happen?

Several days later the salt will begin to 'grow' and cover the stones with beautiful crystals.

What you need

- A plate
- Warm water
- Table salt
- Vinegar

Conclusion

Due to capillary action, the salt water makes its way into the rocks and gradually evaporates leaving behind salt formations. The role of the vinegar is to eliminate greasy spots on the stones which obstruct the flow of the water.

CHEMISTRY

Restoring the lustre of aluminum

The fact

Aluminium pots and pans get tarnished (turn dark) when they are not used for a while. They can be cleaned effectively with pieces of lemon. This is proved through an experiment given below.

What you need

- A tarnished aluminium utensil
- Lemon slices
- Water

How to do the experiment?

1. Pour water into the utensil and warm it on fire.
2. Once the water begins to boil, throw in the lemon slices.

What will happen?

The utensil's colour will become lighter.

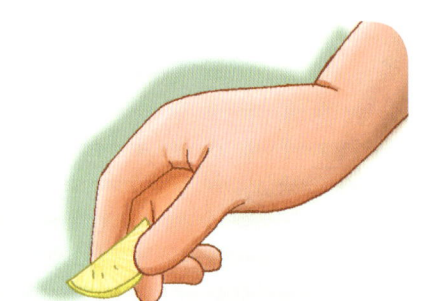

Conclusion

The acid in the lemon reacts with the tarnish to form an aluminium salt which is easily soluble in water.

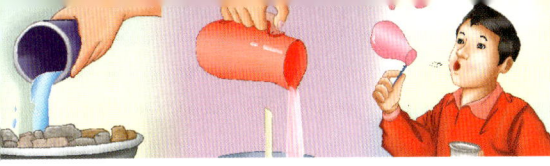
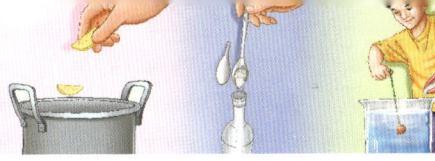

Burning metal

The fact

Metals have characteristic and well-known properties. They are good conductors of heat and electricity, they are malleable, they have lustre etc. Some metals have special properties.

How to do the experiment?

1. Light the candle.
2. Pour the powder slowly with the spoon on to the flame.

What will happen?

The aluminium burns easily and sparkles are formed.

What you need

- Aluminium powder
- A candle
- Match sticks and a spoon

Conclusion

This experiment proves that aluminium does have special properties.

27

CHEMISTRY

Fire needs oxygen to burn

The fact

Fire cannot burn without oxygen. If we seal a burning candle in a glass jar, it will go out after it has used up all the oxygen. Oxygen makes up about one-fifth of the volume of air. We shall prove it with this experiment.

What you need

- A candle
- Plasticine
- A small saucer
- Food colour
- Coins
- A glass jar
- Water

How to do the experiment?

1. Fix the candle vertically on a lump of plasticine in the middle of the saucer.
2. Place four stacks of coins around the candle to form a base for the jar.
3. Pour coloured water (coloured with the food dye) into the saucer to the brim.
4. Ask an adult to light the candle and to place the jar carefully over it.

What will happen?

After a few minutes, the candle will go out and the level of water will rise.

A step further

Compare the duration of burning of different candles in different-sized jars. If they burn longer, then there was more oxygen in the jar.

Conclusion

The flame consumes the oxygen in the jar. As it is consumed, water enters the jar in place of the oxygen. The level of water will reach about one-fifth of the jar. The flame will go out as all the oxygen is consumed.

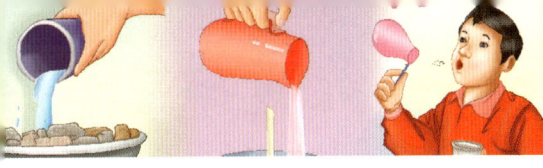 

Heat and margarine

The fact

Stir hot tea with a metal spoon and soon you will feel the spoon getting hot from the tea. This is because the heat has travelled along the spoon from its hot end to its cool end. This kind of heat transfer is called conduction. This experiment will show how this happens.

2. Place them on the end of the three sticks.
3. Put the sticks into the vessel as shown.
4. Pour warm water into the vessel.

What will happen?

The margarine on the metal stick will melt quickly, while that on the other two hardly melts at all.

A step further

Place pieces of chocolate along a spike and heat one end with a candle flame. The heat conducted through the metal melts the pieces one by one. You will soon see that you will not be able to hold the spike without using a cork stopper at the end as the end will turn very hot.

What you need

- Three identically sized sticks made out of wood, any metal and plastic
- Margarine
- A knife
- A kitchen utensil (pot or pan)
- Some warm water

How to do the experiment?

1. Cut out pieces of margarine of equal size.

Conclusion

Metals are good conduct of heat, while wood and plastic are poor conductors of heat.

29

CHEMISTRY

Salt melts ice

The fact

Salt helps to melt ice. The following experiment will show this.

What you need

- A glass of water
- An ice-cube
- Some thin string
- Salt

How to do the experiment?

1. Put the ice in the water.
2. Moisten the string and let it lie across the ice-cube.
3. Sprinkle a little salt across the string and the exposed side of the ice.

What will happen?

The ice around the string will begin to melt, but soon it will re-freeze together with the string. Now pick up the ends of the string and lift the ice-cube out of the glass.

Conclusion

Salt causes the ice to melt. In this process, the ice loses heat but the cold ice-cube soon causes the salty water to freeze, whereby the string is trapped inside the ice. For this reason if there is ice on the roads in winter, a lot of salt needs to be used in order to make sure that all the ice is melted.

Soap vs detergent

The fact

Soaps do not lather well with hard water while detergents do. The following experiment will show us how.

What you need

- Measuring spoons
- Epsom salts
- Measuring cup
- Water
- 1/4 teaspoon of grated soap
- Any detergent
- Two glasses

How to do the experiment?

1. Dissolve 1 tablespoon of Epson salts in 2 cups of water. This makes "hard" water.
2. Put 5 tablespoons of "hard" water in each of the glasses.
3. Put 1/4 teaspoon of grated soap in one glass and label it 'soap'.
4. Put 1/4 teaspoon of detergent in the second glass and label it 'detergent'.
5. Cover the top of the glass with the palm of your hand and shake twenty times.

What will happen?

You should see a marked difference between the amount of foam produced by the detergent and the amount produced by soap. The detergent will produce more foam as compared to the soap.

Conclusion

Detergents are not affected by the presence of minerals in hard water while soaps do not foam well with hard water.

Index

A
alcohol 19

B
Bicarbonate of soda 23

C
capillary 21, 25
casein 17
conduction 29
cream of tartar 13

D
density 7, 15, 25

E
Epson salts 16, 31
evaporation 4, 24

G
glycerine 6, 24

H
hydrocarbons 6

I
indicator 12, 13
inertia 15
intermolecular attraction 21, 25

M
membrane 8, 18
molecules 4, 8, 15

N
neutral 13

P
porous 9, 25

R
reinforcement 14
residues 8

S
saturated solution 16
Sodium Acetate 23
stalactite 16
styrofoam 5
surface tension 8, 9, 18

T
tarnish 26

V
vinegar 12, 13, 17, 23, 25

PEGASUS ENCYCLOPEDIA LIBRARY

Experiments and Activities
NATURE

Edited by: Aparna Chatterji
Managing editor: Tapasi De
Designed by: Vijesh Chahal and Anil Kumar
Illustrated by: Suman S. Roy, Tanoy Choudhury
Colouring done by: Vinay Kumar, Sonu, Kiran Kumari & Pradeep Kumar

CONTENTS

Introduction 3
Acid Rain 4
Making an ant farm 6
Tornado in a bottle 8
A home for toads 10
Can evaporation be stopped? 11
Talking to plants makes them grow 12
Growing bacteria 14
Growing plants from seeds 16
Making a pond 17
Rock candy 18
Colour of apple 19
A kitchen garden 20
Make clean water 21
Potatoes that float 22
Make a river 23
Dipping in the pond 24
Layers of soil 25
Your backyard neighbours 26
New plants from old plants 27
Making craters 28
A wavy activity 30
Fossil cast 31
Index 32

Introduction

Learning and experiencing new things is a continuous process. Children are much more inquisitive than we elders are. They are always bubbling with enthusiasm when it comes to knowing new things. That is the reason they are so full of questions. This enthusiasm should never be curbed; instead, it should be encouraged!

It is a proven fact that children learn the most by doing, experiencing and seeing things. Teaching them through books and worksheets only, does not suffice. We all know that 'seeing is believing'.

But sometimes due to the constraint of time and many other factors, elders are not successful in giving those experiences and exposure to their children which they deserve.

This encyclopedia on Nature is full of activities and experiments related to nature. It will act as a guide, a teacher and help children in increasing their scientific knowledge. Most of the activities and experiments mentioned here can be done by children alone.

This particular encyclopedia will not only teach children many new things about nature but will also make them better citizens as they will become more concerned about their planet Earth!

The first Japanese car in the United States was the Honda Accord manufactured in November 1982.

NATURE

Acid Rain

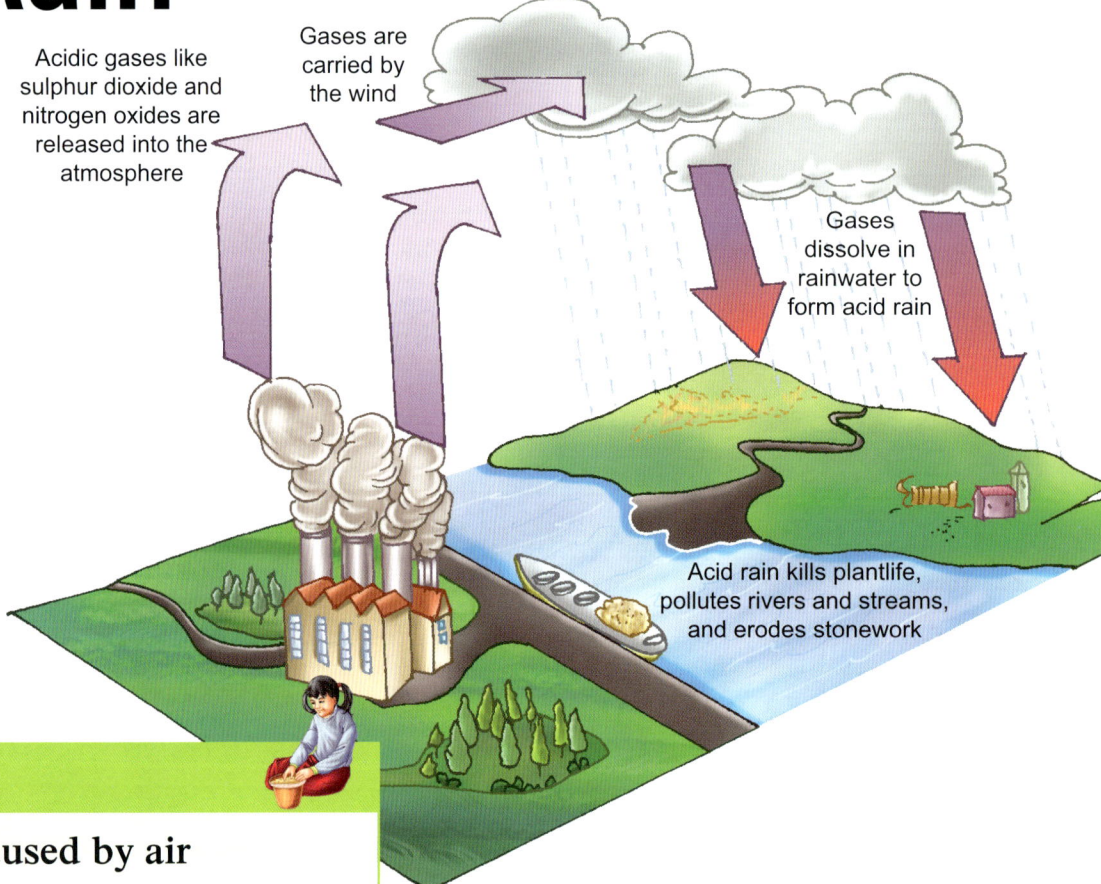

Acidic gases like sulphur dioxide and nitrogen oxides are released into the atmosphere

Gases are carried by the wind

Gases dissolve in rainwater to form acid rain

Acid rain kills plantlife, pollutes rivers and streams, and erodes stonework

The fact

Acid rain is caused by air pollutants in the atmosphere. These pollutants are formed due to the smoke from factories, industries and the exhaust of vehicles. Many other pollutants contribute to acid rain as well. The pollutants gather in dense clouds and fall back to Earth when it rains. The pollutants which are acidic, effect the growth of plant life negatively. Let us see how through this experiment.

What you need

- Three jars with lids
- Three growing bean plants in small cups or small separate planting pots
- Masking tape
- Marking pen
- Lemon juice
- Water
- Tablespoon

Acid Rain

How to do the experiment?

1. Label each bean plant container as 'A', 'B', and 'C'.

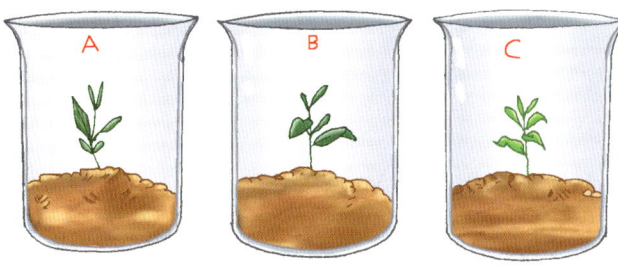

2. Then, label the three jars with masking tape 'A', 'B', and 'C'.

3. Pour 1/2 cup of lemon juice into jar 'A'.
4. Pour 1/4 cup lemon juice into jar 'B'.
5. Don't put any lemon juice into jar 'C'.
6. Add 1/2 cup of water to each jar (A, B, C).
7. Place the growing bean plants on a windowsill where there is sufficient sunlight.
8. Water each plant with four tablespoons of the solution marked for that particular plant (that is, plant 'A' gets solution 'A', plant 'B' gets solution 'B', plant 'C' gets solution 'C').

What will happen?

Plant 'A' will show the effects of acid rain first. The leaves will begin to curl and shrivel. Its growth will slow down or stop completely. It will begin to look sickly. Next plant 'B' will start to show the effects of acid rain but at a slower pace. Plant 'C' will remain healthy because it received no acid rain at all.

Conclusion

The acid in the lemon juice retards the growth of the plants just like the acids of the acid rain.

Making an ant farm

Ants are tiny creatures who are known for their hard working nature and their discipline. Let us learn through this activity how to make an ant farm and have a closer look at the lives of these tiny creatures.

The Ant farm is a very useful and entertaining toy for all ages. One can see the world's tiniest engineers dig tunnels, build roads, erect bridges, and go about their 'chores' around the farmhouse.

What you need

- Ant farm
- A vial full of ants
- Coloured sand meant for the ant farm

How to do the activity?

1. Place the ant farm on a table.
2. Pour the sand into the observation tank. If you have coloured sand, then place it in layers. The ant food is already mixed in the sand.
3. Now wet the sand with a little water. Dampen the whole sand, but don't over do it. You may use a medicine dropper to add the water evenly.
4. Let the wet sand settle for a day or two, keep the lid open to allow excess water to evaporate. The wet sand makes it easier for the ants to dig tunnels.
5. Before putting the ants, you may add some extra food to the sand though it already contains some ant food. You may add things like a small piece of a fruit or a piece of damp bread.
6. Now you may add the ants to complete the farm. But first put the vial containing the ants in the refrigerator for 2-3 minutes. This calms them down while still in the vial. Do not leave them in the freezer for more than 3 minutes. Next, tap the vial with the ants into the farm. Quickly close the lid.

What will happen?

The ants will be busy eating, carrying load and digging tunnels.

Astonishing fact

Did you know that ants are capable of carrying objects 50 times their own body weight with their mandibles.

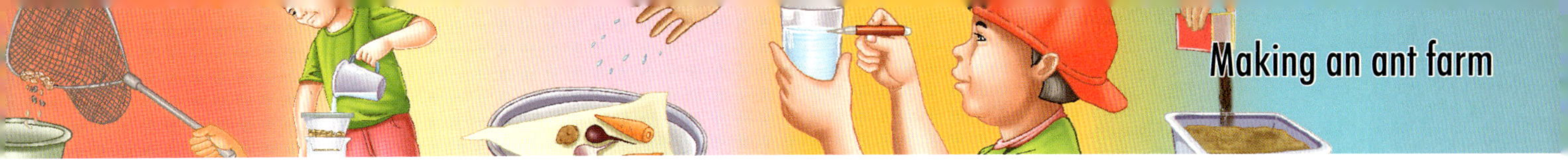

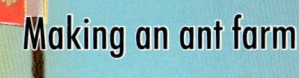

What will you learn?

The ants can be an inspiration to you due to their hard working nature and sense of discipline. You will be surprised how they walk in a perfect queue and how they gather food for odd times!

NATURE

Tornado in a bottle

The fact

A tornado is a violent rotating column of air extending from a thunderstorm to the ground. They are commonly known as twisters. They can cause tremendous destruction by destroying large buildings, uprooting trees and hurling vehicles. Let us see how to make a tornado in a bottle.

What you need

- 2 plastic bottles with capacity of 1 litre each
- Water
- Food colour
- Small styrofoam balls (Optional)
- Small washer 1/4"
- Duct tape

Tornado in a bottle

How to do the activity?

1. Fill one of the empty bottles with water.
2. Add a few drops of food colour to the water.
3. Add the small styrofoam balls also.
4. Put the 1/4 inch washer on top of the filled bottle.
5. Now invert the other bottle on top of it so they are connected. Use the duct tape to make the joint, water tight.
6. Now turn the bottle with the water upside down so that the water is on top and watch how quickly the water gushes to the lower bottle forming a twister.

NATURE

A home for toads

In this fun nature activity, let us make a toad shelter for our friendly backyard neighbours who eat lots of insects.

curved side up as a toad shelter. Cover the ground beneath the pot with moist moss and leaves.

2. Make sure you place the pot near an area where there is plenty of water. Then wait for the toads to arrive. After a while, you will notice toads coming and sitting under your pot resting and eating bugs!

What you need

- A big, broken ceramic flower pot or bowl
- Mosses and soft leaves

How to do the activity?

1. Turn the broken pot or bowl with the

What will you learn?

You can observe the behaviour of the toads very closely; that is, which are the insects that the toads generally eat and how they interact with each other.

Can evaporation be stopped?

The fact

We all know that water constantly evaporates from the seas, lakes, rivers and ponds. But it is possible to stop evaporation, which we will show by this experiment.

What you need

- A glass
- A saucer
- A marker of any colour

How to do the experiment?

1. Draw a line around half-way up the glass.
2. Fill with water up to the line.
3. Pour the water from the glass into the saucer. Now pour more water into the glass up to the line. In this manner, there will be equal quantities of water in both the glass and the saucer.
4. Cover the glass with another saucer and leave the saucer filled with water, outside.
5. Leave them untouched for a day.

What will happen?

Most of the water in the saucer will have evaporated, while the level of the water in the glass will remain unchanged.

Conclusion

Water evaporates to form water vapour. If this water vapour is carried away by air, then water would continue to evaporate. However, if the water vapour is not carried away by the air, then an equilibrium is reached and there is no further increase in the amount of water vapour formed.

Talking to plants makes them grow

The fact

The renowned Indian scientist Jagdish Chandra Bose discovered that plants responded to any kind of stimuli just like animals. His experiments proved that plants grow faster in pleasant music and their growth slows down in noise!

What you need

- 4 small pots of the same size with holes on their bottoms
- Some soil to fill them
- Radish seeds
- Some tap water

How to do the experiment?

1. Fill the pots with soil.
2. Moisten the soil with little tap water
3. Sprinkle 8-10 ordinary radish seeds on the soil.
4. Now sprinkle about 1/4 inch of soil over the seeds and put water again. Be careful not to water it too much.
5. Water them lightly every day.
6. After the seeds sprout, place all the pots together, preferably outdoors where there is ample sunlight.
7. Label each pot with a name or number.

Indian Scientist Jagdish Chandra Bose

How will you treat the plants?

1. Ignore one pot of plants. Never pick it up or give it any attention.
2. Say 'hello', smile and say a few nice words every day to the second plant for about 15 seconds.
3. Behave similarly with the third plant also, but spend about 1 minute speaking soft and nice words of affection. The child should also gently touch the leaves.
4. Treat the fourth plant very kindly. Fawn over the plant in words and gestures. Gently stroke the leaves and speak with much affection. Spend as much time per as you can. Each session should be of 2 minutes.

What will happen?

Generally, radishes mature in 35-45 days. When you review the plants after this period you will see that all the 4 plants have different growth levels. You may note the differences in plant size, leaf colour and taste. The plants to whom you have shown affection will surely show higher growth rate than the others.

Conclusion

Plants do respond better when they are talked to and when affection is shown just like animals.

Growing bacteria

The fact

Bacteria are a fascinating type of microorganism that play quite an important role in our lives. Let us grow our own sample of bacteria and see how it reproduces in a short span of time.

How to do the experiment?

1. Prepare your petrie dish of agar.

2. Using your cotton buds, swab any area of your house that is, collect a sample by rubbing the cotton bud on a surface of your choice (like kitchen sink or bathroom wash basin).

3. Rub the swab over the agar with a few gentle zig zag strokes before putting the lid back on the petrie dish.

4. Keep the dish in a warm area for 2 or 3 days.

5. Check the growth of bacteria each day by making an observational drawing and describing the changes.

6. Dispose off the bacteria by wrapping up the petrie dish in an old newspaper and placing it in the dustbin.

What you need

- Petrie dish of agar
- Cotton buds
- Some old newspaper

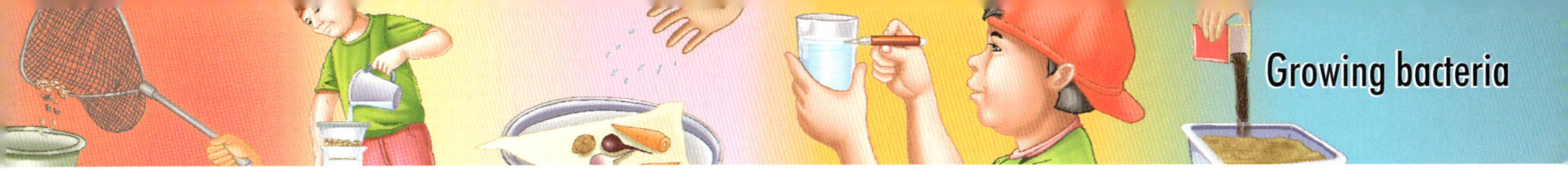

Growing bacteria

Warning

Do not open the lid while throwing.

Note: A Petri dish is a shallow glass or plastic lidded dish that scientists use to culture cells or small mosses. It was named after the German bacteriologist Julius Richard Petri, who invented it.

What will happen?

The agar plate and warm conditions provided the ideal conditions for the bacteria to grow. The bacteria on the plate grow into colonies, each a clone of the original. They steadily grow and become visible to the naked eye in a relatively short time. Different samples produce different results. You will find bacteria throughout the Earth; it grows in soil, radioactive waste, water, on plants and even animals too.

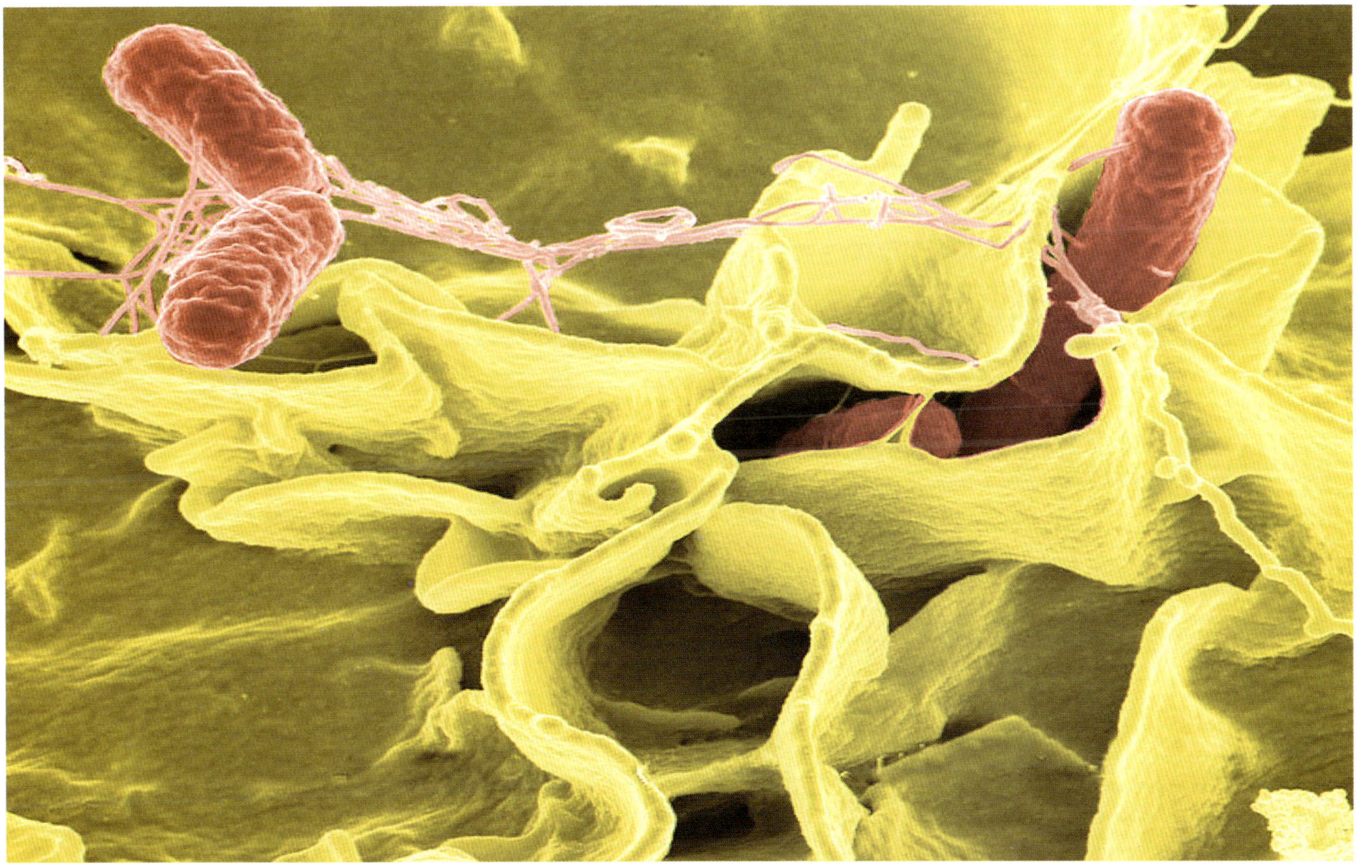

A step further

Try repeating the process with a new petrie dish and swab from under your finger nails or between your toes.

15

NATURE

Growing plants from seeds

The fact

When given the right temperature, sunlight and water, seeds grow into young seedlings. Let us grow our own seedling and monitor its growth though this experiment.

What you need

- Pumpkins seeds or sunflower seeds
- Good quality soil (you can also buy some potting soil from your local garden store)
- A pot to hold the soil and your seeds
- Water
- sunlight

How to do the experiment?

1. Fill the pot with soil.
2. Plant the seeds inside the soil.
3. Place the pot in some place where there is sunlight though try to avoid too much direct sunlight; a window sill is a good place for this.
4. Keep the soil moist by watering it everyday but do not water it too much.
5. Record your observations.

What will happen?

After a week of care, the seeds will germinate and tiny seedlings will sprout.

Making a pond

A pond is body of water smaller than a lake. Let us make a pond by ourselves and see how many animals we can attract to it.

What you need

- A flat tray
- Gravel
- Soil
- Large stones
- Some water plants such as pond weed

Visitors you may have

Mosquito

Turtle

Snails

Frogs

Dragon flies

How to do the activity?

1. Cover the tray with gravel and some soil. Put a big stone in the middle to make an island.
2. Now fill the tray with rain water as it is best for a pond.
3. Place the plants fixing them with stones and soil.
4. Make a chart of your pond. Note which animals visit your pond and where they stay. Make comparisons from day to day.

Rock candy

We all love to eat candies, don't we? Let's make one at home! It only requires a few simple ingredients and just a little time and patience.

What you need

- 15cm piece of string
- A pencil
- A paper clip (or large plastic bead)
- 1 cup of water
- 2 cups of sugar
- A glass jar

How to do the experiment?

1. Tie the 15cm piece of string to the middle of the pencil.
2. Tie the paper clip (or bead) onto the end of the string.
3. Put the pencil across the top of a jar so that the string hangs down into the middle of the jar.
4. If it hangs down too far into the jar, roll the string around the pencil until the string withdraws a little. The string should not touch the sides or bottom of the jar. The string with the bead or the paper clip will act as a seed for the crystal.
5. Now the string and the pencil are ready. Remove them from the jar and put them aside.
6. Pour water into a pan and bring it to boil. Pour about 1/4 cup of sugar into the boiling water; stir it until it dissolves.
7. Keep adding more and more sugar, each time stirring it until it dissolves, until no more will dissolve. Such a solution is called a saturated solution.
8. Carefully pour the hot sugar solution into the jar. Then submerge the paper clip or bead tied to the string into the sugar solution. Be sure the string hangs down into the sugar solution.
9. Allow the contents of the jar to cool and put it in someplace where it will not be moved and shaken. In about a week you will have a large crystals to lick!

Colour of apple

The fact

When sliced apple pieces are kept exposed, they turn brown. Then we do not feel like eating them. But we can prevent this very easily. Let us perform this simple experiment and find out how.

What you need

- An apple
- Half a lemon
- Shallow bowl
- Water
- Knife

How to do the experiment?

1. Peel and slice an apple.
2. Place one slice in a shallow bowl full of water.
3. Smear the second slice with the juice of half a lemon.
4. Leave the third slice exposed to air.
5. Wait for an hour; then compare.

What will happen?

The slice with nothing on it turns brown.

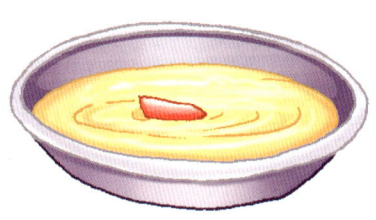

Conclusion

When an apple is cut open, chemicals inside the apple combine with oxygen from the air to form a brown coating. The coating keeps coming in contact with oxygen which goes deeper into the apple slice. Water prevents the first slice from oxygen in the air; so it remains white. Vitamin C in the lemon juice, contains antioxidents which keep oxygen away from the second slice. So, it stays white for the longest time.

A kitchen garden

The fact

Learning about how plants grow can be simple and interesting. You may observe this process of growing a plant without soiling your hands with mud through a simple activity on your mom's kitchen table! Let us see how.

What you need

- Root vegetables like carrots, parsnips, turnips, beets, potatoes
- Knife and cutting board
- Paper towels
- Shallow dish or plate
- Water

How to do the experiment?

1. Chop the top parts of each vegetable (about 1 inch thick)
2. Place 2 sheets of paper towels on a plate or shallow dish. Wet the sheets with water.
3. Place the vegetable tops on the moist sheets of paper towels.
4. Leave the dish beside a window from where sunlight filters in.
5. Check the paper towel daily to see if its moist and add freshwater when the paper towels start getting dry.

What will happen?

A few days later, the vegetables will sprout looking like a small garden.

Make 'clean water'

Most of us do not think much about the cleanliness of water that we use. This is because we are all used to clean water in our daily lives so naturally we seldom care to think about it. Let us see how you can get clean and pure water through the experiment given below.

What you need

- Gravel
- Sand
- Blotting paper or 3 or 4 coffee filters
- A clean flower pot
- Transparent jug
- Large measuring cup or pouring jug

How to do the experiment?

1. Place blotting paper, sand and finally gravel in a clean flower pot.
2. Place the flower pot in a larger transparent vessel so the filtered water can drip through the hole and the children can see it.
3. In a big measuring cup, put some dirt, bits of plants, leaves and water.
4. Mix it well to make muddy water.
5. Pour the muddy water into the flower pot as shown in the image.

What will happen?

The water will drip from the flower pot and gather into the transparent vessel. This water will be cleaner and clearer.

Conclusion

The layers of sand, gravel and blotting paper act as filters holding back the dirt and helping in filtering the water.

A step further

You may arrange the layers in a different order and compare the colour of the filtered water.

NATURE

Potatoes that float

The fact

It is seen that objects generally float in liquids with higher density than plain water. Let us see this through a simple experiment.

What you need

- Three potato slices
- Three glasses of water
- A spoon
- Salt or sugar

How to do the experiment?

1. Make a concentrated solution of salt or sugar in a glass of water. Number the glass as 1.

2. In the second glass, create a layered mix of sugar or salt water with regular water on top of it. To create a layered mix, pour concentrated sugar syrup into the second glass till it is half filled and then top it up with regular water.

3. Leave the water in the third glass alone.

4. Place potato slices in each glass.

What will happen?

- The slice that is dropped into the first glass will float in the salt solution.
- The potato slice put in the second glass will sink halfway and float in the middle of the glass.
- The last slice will sink to the bottom of the glass.

Conclusion

The first glass had a saturated solution of salt or sugar which was denser than the potato slice. So, the slice floated. The density of the second solution was a little more than the second slice. So the second slice floated in the middle of the glass. But the density of water was less than the potato slice in the third glass. In other words, the potato slice was heavier than the water. So it sank to the bottom of the glass.

Make a river

Rivers are one of the richest and the most fertile sources of water on the surface of the Earth. They are formed when water from rain, melted snow, lakes and springs collects together shaping its way through the Earth. Let us make a mini river and see it meandering.

What you need

- Small stones
- Some soil
- A metal or plastic tray
- A jug of water

How to do the activity?

1. Cover the tray with mud.
2. Place the stones in one corner of the tray.
3. Cover the stones with soil. Shape it in such a manner so that it looks like a hill.
4. Now put some stones on the sides of the hill on top of the soil.
5. Fill the jug with water and pour it on the top of the hill.

What will happen?

The mini river will move forward, down the hill making channels and carrying soil downhill.

What did you learn?

This activity demonstrated the movement of a river and how it carries soil with it.

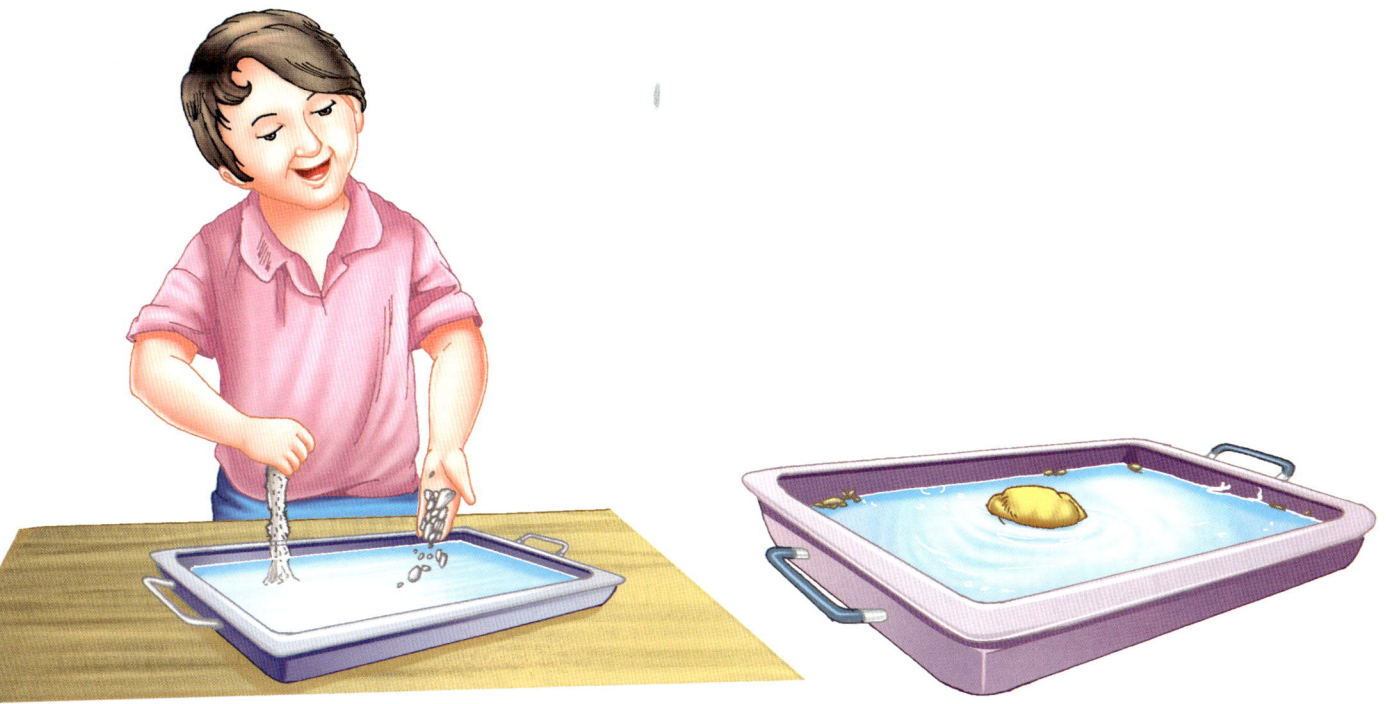

Dipping in the pond

Ponds are water bodies smaller than lakes. Spring and summers are considered to be the best time to go for pond dipping with plastic containers. You will find all kinds of plants and animals living in the pond.

What you need

- A plastic container
- A fine net
- A magnifying glass

How to do the activity?

1. Fill your plastic container with pond water. The container should be cleaned properly before use.
2. Sweep your net in the water of the pond.
3. Empty the contents of the net into another container.
4. With a magnifying glass, examine all the plants and creatures you have caught.
5. Now sweep your net in the middle of the pond. What did you find?

What you may find in the pond

- Sticklebacks
- Great pond snails
- Leeches
- Water boatman
- Mosquitoes

Layers of soil

Soil is an important part of our Earth. It is generally full of minerals and water that plants need for growth. Many tiny creatures like moles and worms also make it their home.

What you need

- Some soil
- A bucket
- A sieve
- A screw-top jar

How to do the activity?

1. Dig up some soil from your backyard and put it in a bucket.
2. Sieve some soil with the help of a sieve onto some paper and see what is left behind. You may find stones, bits of plants or even tiny living creatures in the soil.
3. Now put some soil into a screw-top jar. Fill the jar almost to the top with water and screw on the lid tightly.
4. Shake the jar vigorously until all the contents mix properly; then leave the jar for sometime.
5. After a while, look at the jar carefully. The soil will settle into layers in the water.

NATURE

Your backyard neighbours

There are many small creatures such as spiders, snails, millipedes and slugs that stay in your backyard. Seldom do we think about them. Many a time, we are even scared of them. But did you know that these tiny creatures form a very vital part of our environment? Let us set a trap and try to attract a few of these through this activity.

How to do the activity?

Preparing the trap

1. Dig a hole in the soil deep enough to hold a small container. Fill it with pieces of fruits and a spoonful of cat food and dog food.

2. Cover the hole (trap) with a small stone propped up at one end with another stone so that there is a small gap.

3. Leave the trap overnight. Lift the rock to see what you have caught. Before you let your tiny neighbours leave, try to find out what they are.

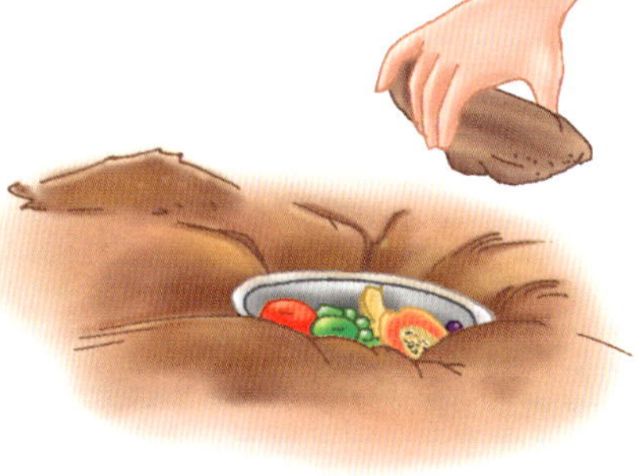

26

New plants from old plants

Plants are generally grown from seeds. But some plants can be grown from old plants without using seeds! A potato is a starchy plant tuber that is packed with food that a new potato plant needs to grow. It has little buds on its surface called eyes. Let us grow new potato plants with the help of old ones through this activity.

What you need

- A potato with eyes or buds
- A shoe box with a lid
- Cardboard
- Scissors
- Tape

How to do the activity?

1. Bend the end of each strip of cardboard to make a flap. Tape the flaps to the sides of the box to make a maze.

2. Place the potato in the box and put on the lid. After a few days, shoots will start to grow from the eyes through the maze towards the light.

What will happen?

A potato plant will grow from a piece of a potato bulb.

Making craters

Meteors, and comets are heavenly bodies which sometimes hurl at great speeds and collide with the surface of the Earth. It is then that they form holes or craters on the Earth's surface. Let us make such craters and see what are the factors that affect the size and depth of such craters.

What you need

- Flour (or sand or soil)
- 1 cup hot chocolate powder or cocoa
- A big, deep container
- Ruler
- Small, medium and large marbles or rocks, ping pong or golf balls
- A string of 1.5 metres
- Drop cloth, newspaper or any other floor covering

How to do the experiment?

1. Spread the drop cloth or newspaper or try this outside as this experiment maybe a little messy.

2. Place the container in the middle of the drop cloth and fill the tray three inches high with flour (or sand or soil). Make sure the flour is spread evenly across the pan.

3. Now, sprinkle a thin, even layer of hot chocolate powder on top.

4. Now sit close to the tray. Gather the impactors (marbles or rocks), string and ruler.

5. Make craters in the following way
   - Mark the string at 30 cm and again at 1.5m.
   - Roughly calculate the diameter of each of your impactors using a ruler.

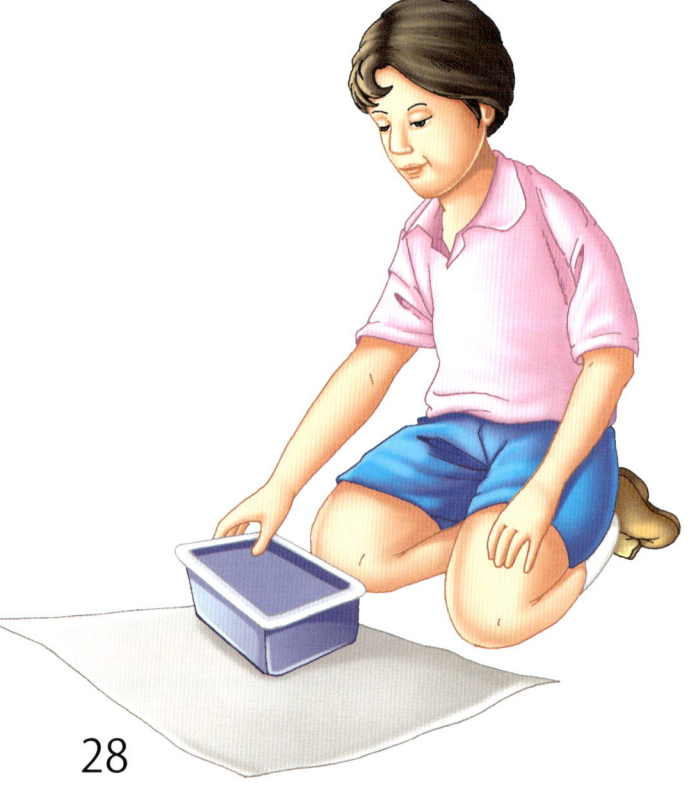

Making craters

- Take a note and see which impactors are heavier than the others.
- Drop the first impactor from a height of 30 cm.
- Measure the diameter and depth of the crater it forms. Record your findings.
- Drop the first impactor again from a height of 1.5 m. Be sure to drop it away from your first crater. Record your findings.
- Repeat these steps with the other impactors.

What will happen?

Different impactors will form craters of different sizes and depths.

What did you learn?

When comets and asteroids collide with planets, they create impact craters. The size and depth of impact craters increase with the size, speed and travelling distance of these heavenly bodies. The bigger the object and the faster it travels, the bigger the crater. This is because bigger and faster meteors release more energy when they collide with another body.

NATURE

A wavy activity

Let us find out how liquids of different densities interact and let us form wavy patterns with this experiment.

What you need

- Clear plastic bottle with a tight cap
- Water
- Food colour
- Mineral oil

How to do the activity?

1. Fill half the plastic bottle with water.
2. Add blue or green food colour until the water gets dark.
3. Now add mineral oil until the container overflows just a little.
4. Close the cap tightly on.
5. Now tilt the bottle on its side, rock it gently and watch the waves that form. Keep the bottle rocking and continue observing the wavy patterns. Can you make the waves 'collide'?

What will happen?

When the bottle is static, you will see that the oil stands on top of the water. This happens because oil is less dense than water. As you rock the bottle, you will see the wavy patterns. If you rock the bottle with varying force you will create different patterns of waves.

Fossil cast

Fossils are not only interesting records of the past, but they are also beautiful to look at. In this activity you can make a fossil mold or cast in just a few hours. Your fossil cast will have the same details and delicate patterns that a real fossil has.

What you need

- A chunk of plasticine clay (about the size of your fist)
- Dull table knife
- 2 paper cups; bottom should be 25 to 6 cm in diameter
- A sea shell or a small bone
- About 1/2 cup of plastic of Paris
- 1/4 cup of water
- Spoon

How to do the activity?

1. Take a half of clay and flatten it until its about 2.5cm thick and smooth at the top. Trim the circle of the clay until it fits the bottom of the cup.

2. Slide the clay into the cup, flat side up. Carefully press the shell or bone into the clay. Then carefully lift the object out of the clay. You will be able to see an impression of the object.

3. Pour the plaster of Paris into the other cup. Add water and stir til the mixture is smooth.

4. After two to three mixtures pour the mixture into the other paper cup right on top of the clay. Let it sit for on hour without touching it.

5. After an hour, carefully tear away the sides of the paper cup and remove the clay and plaster. Holding the clay part in one hand and the plaster part with the other hard, gently separate them.

6. Use the knife to carefully trim away any rough edges from the plaster fossil cast. Smooth out the edges, the let it dry for a day or two. Your fossil print is now ready.

Index

A

acid rain 4, 5
agar 14, 15
atmosphere 4

B

bacteria 14
blotting paper 21

C

channels 23
comets 28, 29
craters 28, 29
crystal 18

D

density 22

G

germinate 16
gravel 17, 21

M

magnifying glass 24
meteors 28, 29
microorganism 14

P

parsnips 20

Petrie dish 14, 15
pollutants 4

R

radioactive 15
reproduces 14

S

sprout 12, 16, 20
Sticklebacks 24
stimuli 12
styrofoam 8, 9
submerge 18

T

temperature 16
tornado 8
transparent 21

W

Water boatman 24

PEGASUS ENCYCLOPEDIA LIBRARY

Experiments and Activities
PHYSICS

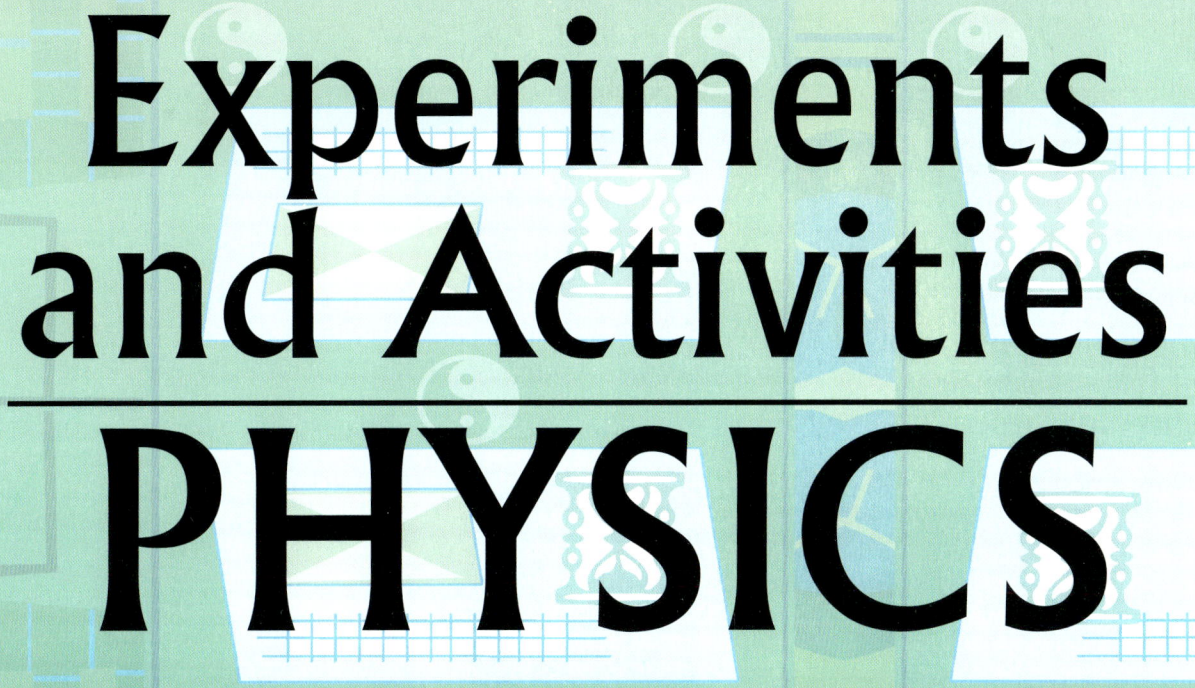

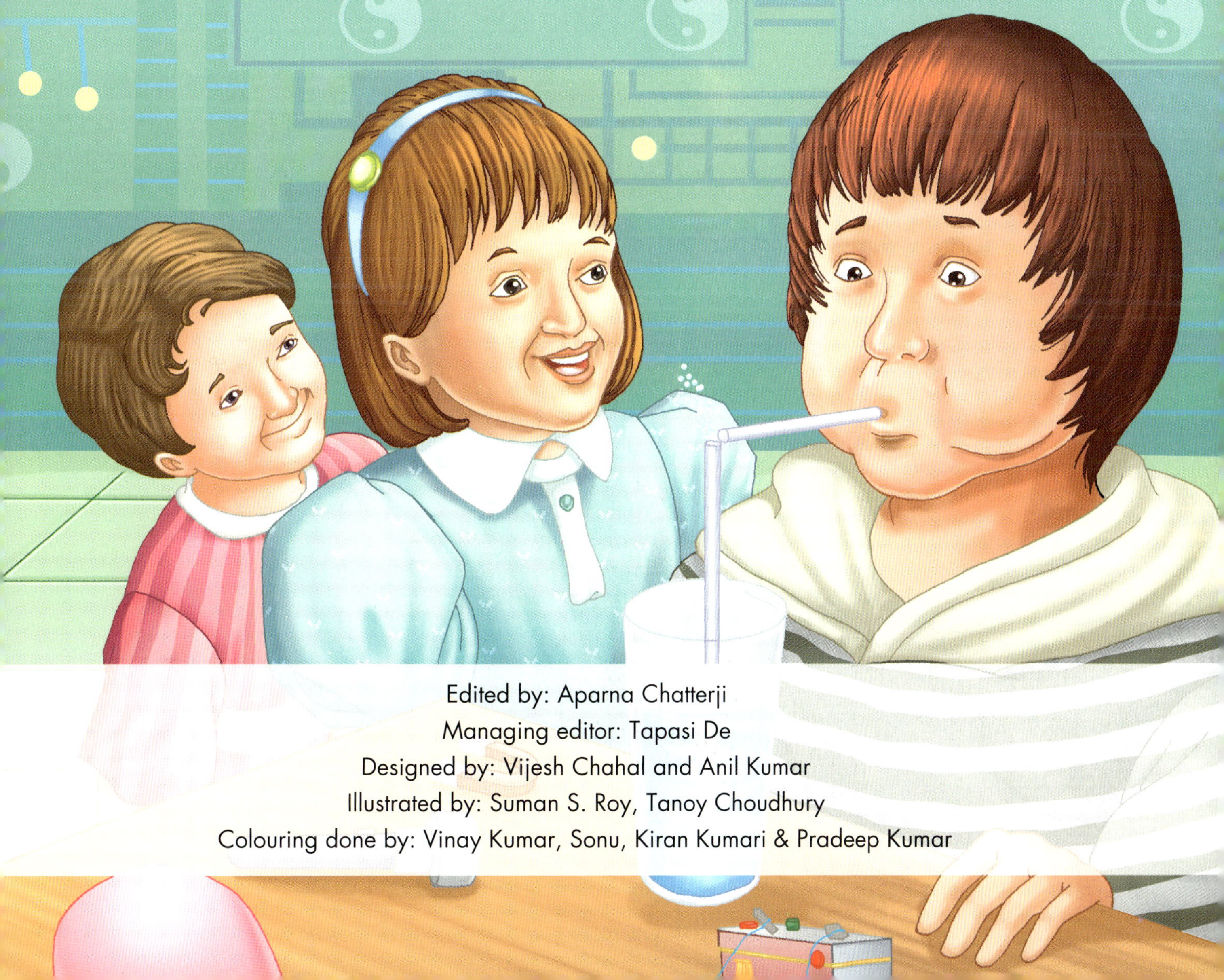

Edited by: Aparna Chatterji
Managing editor: Tapasi De
Designed by: Vijesh Chahal and Anil Kumar
Illustrated by: Suman S. Roy, Tanoy Choudhury
Colouring done by: Vinay Kumar, Sonu, Kiran Kumari & Pradeep Kumar

PHYSICS

CONTENTS

Introduction	3
Which falls faster?	4
Plasticine and coins	5
Making a spray jet	6
Black and white	7
Creating multiple images of an object	8
Finding the centre of gravity	9
Properties of light	10
Convex mirrors and convex lenses	11
Vary the tone	12
Pictures of your voice	13
Singing bottles	14
Tolling bells	15
A hovering paper clip	16
Electricity and magnets	17
Electricity in your hair	18
Dancing under glass	19
Reflection of sound	20
Working of a camera	21
Merging colours	22
Mysterious mirror	23
Ribbons show airflow	24
Expanding a balloon	25
Can metal be extended?	26
Does air have any weight?	27
Fountains at home	28
Lightning from a spoon	29
What absorbs more heat?	30
A flying ping pong ball	31
Index	32

Introduction

Learning and experiencing new things is a continuous process. Children are much more inquisitive than we elders are. They are always bubbling with enthusiasm when it comes to knowing new things. That is the reason they are so full of questions. This enthusiasm should never be curbed; instead, it should be encouraged!

It is a proven fact that children learn the most by doing, experiencing and seeing things. Teaching them through books and worksheets only, does not suffice. We all know that 'seeing is believing'.

But sometimes due to the constraint of time and many other factors, elders are not successful in giving those experiences and exposure to their children which they deserve.

This encyclopedia on Physics helps the young readers to understand their surroundings better. It is full of experiments and activities that give knowledge about the common things of life like light, sound, air, gravity and the numerous other things that a child should know in order to cope up with his surroundings better. This series can be a proud possession of any child who is interested to enhance his practical knowledge.

PHYSICS

Which falls faster?

The fact
Two objects of varying size and weight would hit the ground at the same time when dropped from the same height, provided there is no air resistance.

What will happen?
In the first case the metal plate will reach the floor first, and in the second they will arrive together.

What you need
- A metal plate
- A paper plate

How to do the experiment?
1. Hold both the plates horizontally. Let them fall at the same time.
2. Now place the metal plate over the paper plate and let them fall together.

Conclusion
The metal plate and the paper both fall under the influence of the Earth's gravitational force, but in the first case the metal plate falls faster than the paper plate as it has a higher mass per surface area. The paper plate has lower mass per surface area due to which the resistance from air slows down its fall to a greater extent as compared to the metal plate.

In the second case the metal plate and the paper plate encounter the same resistance; hence, they hit the ground at the same time.

Plasticine and coins

What you need

- Two identical coins
- A plasticine lump

How to do the experiment?

1. Place one coin (horizontally) on the plasticine and press it down with your finger.

2. Now place the other coin on the plasticine sideways (vertically) on its edge and repeat the experiment.

What will happen?

The second coin (one which is placed vertically) will sink into the plasticine much deeper than the first. Plasticine, is a type of modelling clay, a putty-like modelling material made from calcium salts, petroleum jelly and aliphatic acids.

Conclusion

The area of contact of the second coin with the plasticine was much lesser than that of the first. So, the pressure it exerted was also higher and so it sank deeper into the plasticine than the first coin.

Making a spray jet

The fact

An atomizer is a device which converts a stream of liquid into a fine spray. Atomizers mix air with the liquid via a pumping mechanism.

What you need

- A plastic drinking straw
- A glass of water
- A penknife

How to do the experiment?

1. Cut the straw half-way along one third its length.
2. Bend the straw as shown.
3. Immerse the shorter end into the glass and make sure the cut is above the level of the water.
4. Blow air hard through the free end.

What will happen?

Water will enter the straw from the glass and will then be expelled through the slit as a spray.

Conclusion

The strong current of air you have made by blowing reduces the pressure at the top of the immersed part of the straw. The normal pressure acting on the water is now stronger than this reduced pressure, and it forces the water to flow up. The moving air blows the water off in drops.

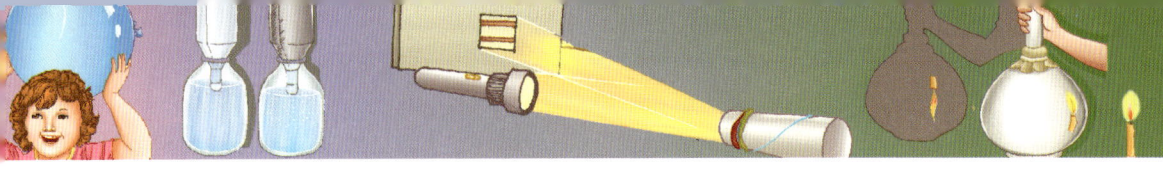

Black and white

The fact

This experiment will tell you that heat reaches objects through radiation.

What you need

- Two identical bottles
- Two identical glass jars
- Water
- Two pieces of paper, one white and one black of identical size and thickness

How to do the experiment?

1. Wrap white paper around one bottle and black paper around the other.
2. Dip their openings into the jars which you have filled with water (as shown).
3. Put both into direct sunlight.

What will happen?

More bubbles of air will be streaming out of the bottle wrapped with black paper.

Conclusion

Black absorbs more radiated heat than white, and the air in the bottle with the black paper will be heated more than that in the other bottle. As it expands, it tries to escape from the bottle.

Now, put the bottles along with the jars in a cool place. Soon you will see that more water has gone into the bottle with the black paper, proving that more air had been displaced from it.

Creating multiple images of an object

The fact

Multiple images can be produced by using two plane mirrors. As the angle between the mirrors decreases, the number of images that can be seen increases.

What you need

- Two books
- Two book-sized plane mirrors
- Two rubber bands
- A pencil

How to do the experiment?

1. Use the rubber bands to fix the mirrors to the books.
2. Place the books upright with the mirrors facing each other.
3. Place the pencil between the books as shown.
4. Look into one mirror and try to see what you can.

What will happen?

You will see numerous images of the pencil on both the mirrors!

Conclusion

The light rays from the pencil bounce many times from one mirror to the other before they reach your eyes.

Finding the centre of gravity

The fact

Centre of gravity of an object is the average location of its weight. Let's find out the centre of gravity of a few things through simple experiments.

What you need

- A book
- A broom
- A ruler
- Other objects

How to do the experiment?

1. Balance a book on your index finger, helping yourself with your other hand until you find the spot where you can easily balance the book horizontally.

2. Hold the broomstick horizontally on both your outstretched index fingers. Slowly move the fingers towards each other, until they meet at the broom's centre of gravity.

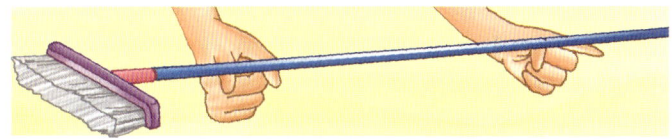

3. Try and balance the broom vertically on your forehead.

4. Try various other objects and find their state of equilibrium.

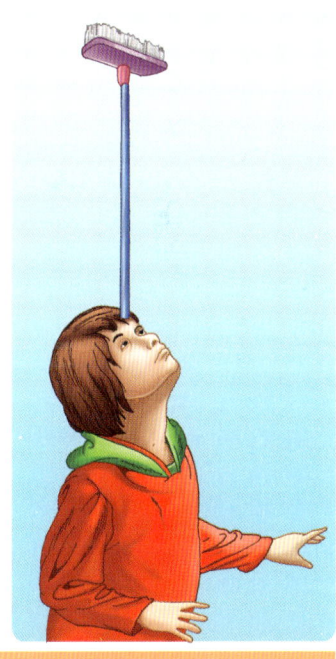

Conclusion

The centre of gravity is an imaginary point about which all the weight (mass) has been evenly distributed in an object. Whenever the centre of gravity lies directly over the base of support, the object remains perfectly balanced and steady.

9

Properties of light

The fact

Rays of light travel at a great speed in a straight line. When they touch our eyes, they convey to us a lot of information about the things around us. This experiment will show just this.

What you need

- Two pieces of cardboard
- A candle
- A pencil
- A ruler
- A sharp cutter

How to do the experiment?

1. Cut out slits vertically on the cardboard pieces and set them up as shown.
2. Make the candle stand right in front of the slit of one of the cardboards. Now light the candle.
3. Now try to see the candle and its flame through the slits of the cardboards.

What will happen?

The flame will be visible to your eye.

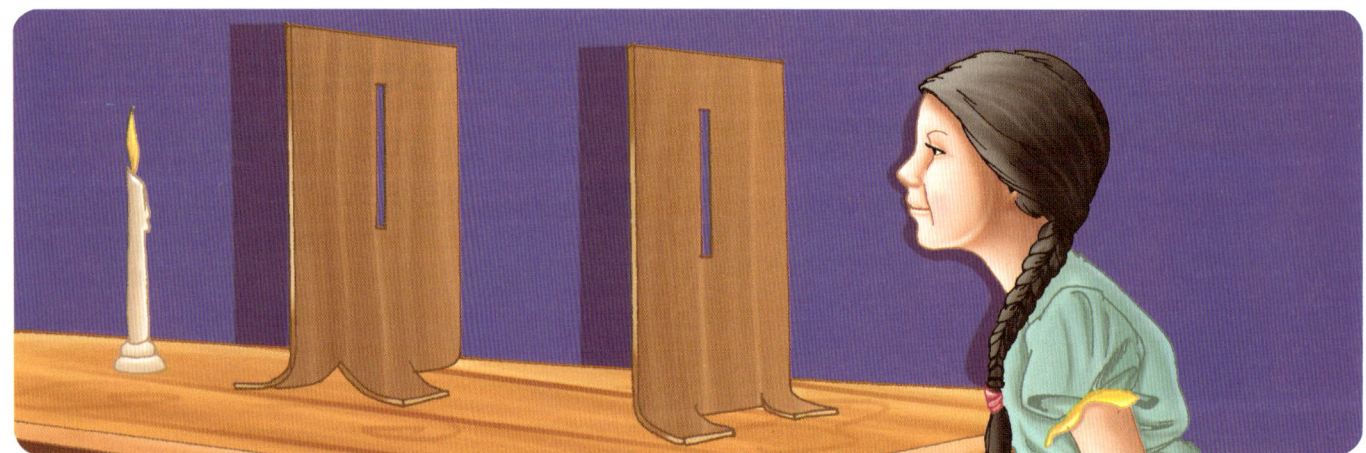

Conclusion

When the candle, both the slits on the cardboards and your eye are in a straight line, only then will the flame of the candle be visible. This is due to the fact that light travels along a straight line.

Convex mirrors and convex lenses

The fact

Images are formed when light rays coming from an object get reflected by a mirror or when they pass through a lens.

What you need

- A spherical glass bottle
- A candle
- Water

How to do the experiment?

1. Fill the bottle with water and hold it between a burning candle and the wall.
2. Keep moving the bottle until you get a sharp image.

What will happen?

You will see a miniature image of the candle on the bottle, while a inverted and magnified image will appear on the wall.

Conclusion

The outer surface of the bottle acts as a convex mirror, which reflects the reduced images of objects. The water in the bottle acts as a convex lens, which produces a inverted and magnified image on the wall.

PHYSICS

Vary the tone

The fact

The pitch of the sound produced by a wire depends on its thickness, length and how tightly it is stretched.

What will happen?

Every change of tension of the wire or distance will produce a different tone.

What you need

- A steel wire
- Two buckets of water,
- Two thin wooden strips

How to do the experiment?

1. Place the strips of wood on a table.
2. Stretch the wire across the strips and tie its ends to the two buckets.
3. Change the tension of the wire by adding water to the buckets and also change the distance between the strips. Pluck the wire.

Conclusion

As the distance between the strips is increased, the length of the wire increases and low pitched sounds are produced. However, the pitch of sound made by the wire does not entirely depend on its length. It also depends on how tightly it is stretched (the tension of the wire). An increase in the tension of the wire produces a corresponding increase in the pitch.

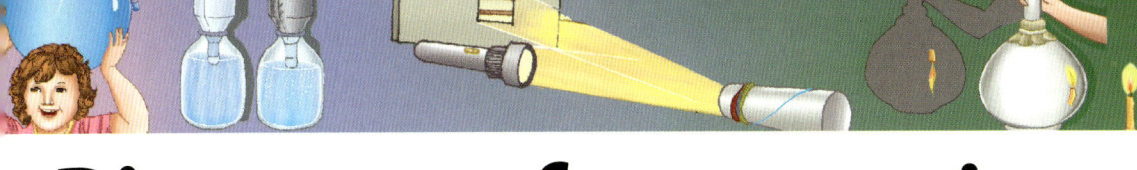

Pictures of your voice

The fact

If you want to see a picture of your voice, try the following experiment.

What you need

- A balloon
- Scissors
- A short cardboard tube
- A rubber band
- Some metal foil
- A flashlight
- Glue

How to do the experiment?

1. Stretch a piece of the balloon rubber tightly across one end of the tube and fix it with the rubber band.
2. Stick a small piece of foil on the balloon rubber.
3. Switch on the flashlight and position it as shown, so that it is pointing at the metal foil at an angle enabling you to see a spot of light reflected on a wall or a piece of paper.
4. Say something into the open end of the tube, changing the pitch and loudness of your voice.

What will happen?

Dashes and wavy lines will appear on the spot of light!

Conclusion

The vibration of your voice makes the air in the tube vibrate. This forces the balloon, foil and therefore also the reflected light to vibrate. You will be able to see this in the form of short lines and wavy lines in the spot of light.

PHYSICS

Singing bottles

The fact

This experiment will show how sound energy can be transferred from one vibrating object to another.

What you need

- Two identical bottles

How to do the experiment?

1. Place the top of a bottle next to your ear.
2. Your friend should stand about one metre away from you and blow across the top of his bottle.

What will happen?

You will hear from your bottle a tone of the same pitch as that coming from the other bottle.

Conclusion

The air vibrations in one bottle induce vibrations in the other, creating a tone of the same pitch but somewhat of lower intensity. This phenomenon is called resonance.

Tolling bells

The fact

The source of sound is typically any vibrating matter. The vibrations then travel away from the source through any medium such as air.

Through this experiment, we will produce a sound that will remind you of tolling bells.

What you need

- A piece of string one metre long
- A fork

How to do the experiment?

1. Tie the fork to the string as shown in the picture.
2. Wind the two ends a few times around your index fingers and put your fingers in your ears.
3. Swing the fork so that it hits a hard object.

What will happen?

You will hear a sound like the tolling of bells.

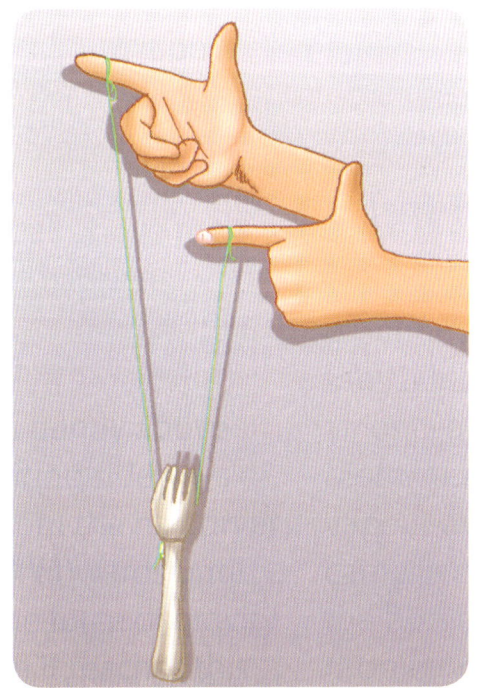

Conclusion

As the fork hits another object, it begins to oscillate. The vibrations are conveyed through the string and your fingers straight to your ear drums.

PHYSICS

A hovering paper clip

The fact

Magnets attract certain types of stainless steel objects too. Stainless steel is an alloy of iron which contains other metals like chromium or nickel. If the steel sample contains only chromium in the mix, then the steel sample would not exhibit magnetic qualities.

What you need

- A steel paper clip (not containing nickel)
- Thread
- Adhesive tape
- A magnet

How to do the experiment?

1. Tie the paper clip to one end of the thread and tape the other end of the thread to the surface of the table.
2. Slowly bring the magnet close to the paper clip.

What will happen?

With a little practice, you will be able to make the clip dance like a cobra.

Conclusion

Stainless steel objects that do not contain nickel are also attracted to magnets.

Electricity and magnets

The fact

Electricity and magnetism have a deep relation. Through this experiment let us show you how. A wire carrying electric current generates a magnetic field around itself.

How to do the experiment?

1. Let the magnetized needle float in the water and tape the wire over it in the same direction in which it is pointing.

2. As soon as you link the wire to a battery, the needle will turn, showing that the conductor through which the electricity is running also acts as a magnet.

What you need

- A magnetized needle on a piece of cork
- A thin wire
- Adhesive tape
- A plateful of water
- An electric battery

Conclusion

As soon as the wire is connected to the battery, electric current starts flowing through it. This generates a magnetic field around the wire which interacts with the magnetic field of the magnetized needle and causes it to turn.

Electricity in your hair

The fact

Static electricity can be produced by rubbing two different materials, specially non metals.

Here is an experiment in which you can use your own hair to make static electricity.

What you need

- String
- Two balloons
- Adhesive tape

How to do the experiment?

1. Stick the string with tape over the two balloons so they are about five to six centimetres apart.
2. Rub one of the balloons on your hair and let it hang next to the other balloon.

What will happen?

The balloons will first attract each other but once they touch they will repel each other.

A step further

Tear a paper tissue into tiny pieces. Rub a balloon on your hair and bring it close to the paper bits, which will then fly up and stick to the balloon.

Conclusion

Rubbing the first balloon with hair caused it to attain negative static charge. Thus, the charged balloon attracted the second balloon which was neutral. However, when the balloons came in contact with each other, charge transfer took place which caused both the balloons to attain negative charge. Hence, the second balloon was repelled.

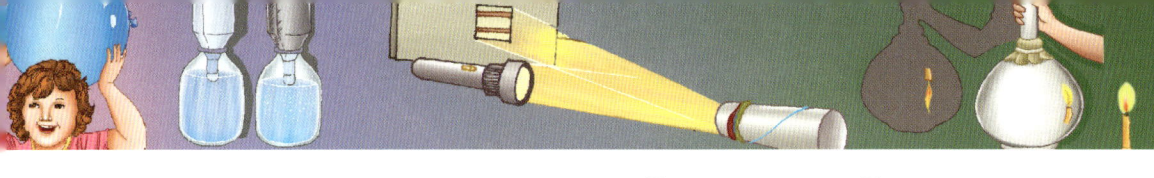

Dancing under glass

The fact
Let us make a puppet theatre which uses static electricity.

What you need
- A piece of glass
- A metal tray
- Aluminium foil
- A silk cloth
- Several large books

How to do the experiment?
1. Cut out several human figures from the foil and place them on the tray.
2. Place 4 books at the 4 corners of the tray and place the glass on top.
3. Rub the glass with the silk cloth. Be careful not to break the glass.

What will happen?
The little men will begin to dance up and down.

Conclusion
Rubbing the glass with cloth charges the glass with static electricity. The charged glass then attracts the figures, to which the charge is then passed. Equal charges repel each other, so the figures then fall off the glass and on to the tray, to which they pass their charges, and then they are attracted up to the glass again.

19

Reflection of sound

The fact

Sound can be reflected from a wall as light from a mirror. Let us see how this happens through this experiment.

What you need

- Old newspapers
- Scissors
- Adhesive tape
- A wind-up clock
- A broomstick

How to do the experiment?

1. Twist a newspaper page tightly around the broomstick. Tape the paper and pull the tube off the stick.
2. Make another tube in similar manner.
3. Hold one tube at an angle towards the wall and place the clock at its end, as shown in the picture.
4. Your friend should point the other tube at the wall and place his or her ear at its end, as shown in the picture.

What will happen?

Your friend will hear the clock clearly.

A step further

Experiment with different positions of the tubes and see how sound is reflected.

Conclusion

The sound waves emitted by the clock travel through the first tube, and strike the wall. The waves are then reflected from the wall and enter the second tube, which carries them to your friend's ear making it possible for him or her to hear the clock ticking.

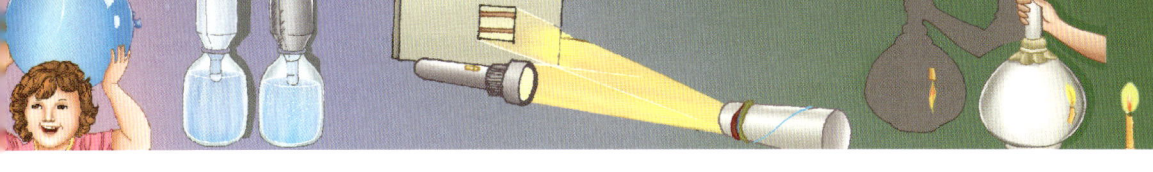

Working of a camera

The fact

A camera is a box which can form an image on a photographic film or on other light-sensitive medium.

What you need

- A small box properly sealed for light
- Translucent paper
- Scissors
- A pin
- Adhesive tape

How to do the experiment?

1. Cut out one of the sides of the box.
2. Replace the missing side with the translucent paper and fix with the tape. Stretch the paper well before fixing it.
3. Make a small hole with the pin in the centre of the side opposite to the translucent paper.
4. Hold up the box with the hole towards a window and move it back and forth slowly.

What will happen?

You will see an upside-down image of the window.

Warning!

1. The camera works best when you aim it at a brightly lit object.
2. In order to be able to see the image displayed on the translucent paper, you need to block out any ambient light. So, it would be advisable to drape an opaque blanket over your head and the camera.

Conclusion

We already know that light travels in a straight line. The rays from the window pass through the hole and hit the paper. Those from the bottom will, therefore, hit the top edge of the paper and those from the top the bottom edge. So, what you will see will be an inverted image of the window.

PHYSICS

Merging colours

The fact

The colour white is a mixture of all the colours. Let us prove this through this experiment.

What you need

- A pencil
- A compass
- Thick white paper
- Scissors
- Paints

How to do the experiment?

1. Make a circle on white paper and cut it out.
2. Divide the circle into segments of equal sizes and paint them with all the colours of a rainbow.
3. Make a small hole in the centre of the circle and pierce it with a pencil.
4. Spin it as fast as you can.

What will happen?

All the colours will merge. If you have painted it with all the colours of a rainbow, the colour you see when you spin the circles will be white.

Note: In case you are unable to observe white colour, you need to spin the wheel faster. You can attach the wheel to a simple motor to make it spin faster.

A step further

Take three flashlights and cover the bulbs with red, blue and green cellophane. In a darkened room, point them at a white wall or a piece of paper. Let the rays mix. How many new colours have you produced?

Conclusion

The circle spins so fast that our eyes cannot see the individual colours but only a mixture of all the colours. White is a mixture of all the colours. So, the colour which will be visible to you will be white.

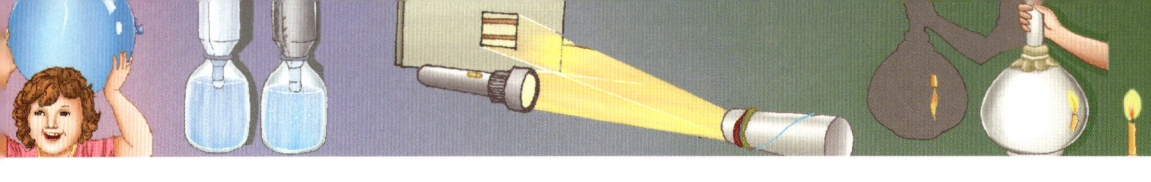

Mysterious mirror

The fact

A mirror image is not an exact copy of the people and things facing the mirror. Let us check.

What you need

- A mirror
- A pencil and some paper

How to do the experiment?

1. Make a drawing of your choice and write its subject underneath.
2. Hold the mirror and your drawing upright against each other.
3. Look at the reflection of your drawing and the letters in the mirror.

What will happen?

The mirror image will be laterally inverted. So will the letters and you may not be able to read your inscription.

A step further

Make 2 mirrors stand facing each other. Keep a small object between them. Look at the mirrors and you will see an endless row of images on both the mirrors.

Conclusion

Rays of light travel in a straight direction unless they hit an obstacle from which they reflect. Light from the sun, a candle's flame and electric bulbs hits our eyes directly, but we see most other things with the help of the light from other sources which hits those things and is then reflected to our eyes.

Polished surfaces such as mirrors reflect light very well. But when you look at yourself in a mirror, you see the left side of the face on the right and the right side on the left. The face you see in the mirror is not the same face others see when they look at you directly. The same goes for other objects, except that you can compare their mirror images with the originals, but you cannot do so with your own face.

PHYSICS

Ribbons show airflow

The fact

Heat energy is transmitted in the form of airflow. Let us see how through this experiment.

What you need

- Thin sheets of paper
- Adhesive tape
- Scissors
- A warm room and a cool room next to it

How to do the experiment?

1. Cut long ribbons from the paper.
2. Stick one end of the ribbons along the top and bottom edge of a door.
3. Open the door slightly.

What will happen?

The ribbons will fly in the opposite directions. The ones at the top of the door will fly from the warm room towards the cold room and the ones at the bottom from the cold room to the warm one.

A step further

Stick a ribbon half-way up the door. Will it move?

Conclusion

Warm air is lighter than cold air and always rises to the upper part of the room. As you open a door, it streams out causing the ribbons at the top to fly towards the cold room. On the other hand, cold air streams into the warm room to replace the warm air through the lower end of the doorway. This causes the ribbons at the bottom to fly towards the warm room.

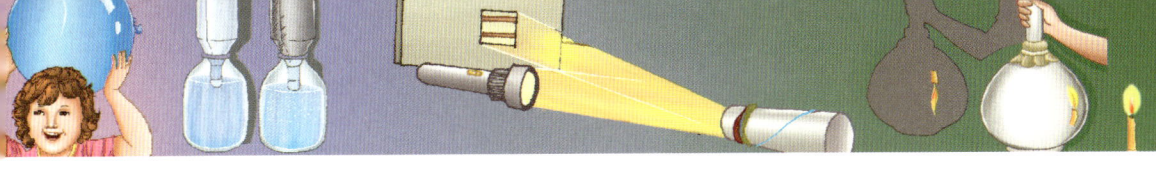

Expanding a balloon

The fact

Gases expand on heating. The size of the balloon can be increased without blowing air into it. Let's check how.

What will happen?

The balloon will gradually expand until it bursts.

What you need

- A balloon
- A candle

How to do the experiment?

1. Place the balloon next to a burning candle and watch what happens.

Conclusion

The air molecules move faster and faster under the influence of heat and the air present inside the balloon expands until the balloon bursts.

PHYSICS

Can metal be extended?

The fact

We know that solids expand when heated. Let us see how.

What you need

- Two bottles
- A cork stopper
- A long aluminium knitting needle
- A sewing needle
- A candle
- A piece of paper
- Scissors

How to do the experiment?

1. Stick the knitting needle into the cork with which you have already plugged one of the bottles.

2. Place the other end of the needle across the top of the other bottle as shown in the picture.

3. Make a paper arrow and pierce it with the sewing needle in the middle.

4. Place the needle with the arrow on top of the bottle which does not have the cork on top.

5. Heat the knitting needle with the candle.

What will happen?

The paper arrow will rotate as you heat the knitting needle.

Conclusion

The knitting needle expands and gets longer due to the heat thus it turns the sewing needle, rotating the arrow as well.

Does air have any weight?

The fact

It is true that air has weight and exerts pressure on the objects with which it is in contact. This simple experiment will prove it.

What will happen?

The water will stay in the glass and the cardboard will not fall off.

What you need

- A glass of water
- A piece of smooth shiny and firm cardboard

How to do the experiment?

1. Cover the glass of water with the cardboard. Holding the cardboard against the rim of the glass, carefully turn it upside down.
2. Slowly remove your hand.

Conclusion

This happens because air exerts its pressure from all directions. Its upward pressure against the cardboard is sufficient to keep the water in the glass.

PHYSICS

Fountains at home

The fact
A liquid's weight produces hydrostatic pressure, which acts in all directions. Let us show this through this experiment.

What you need
- Two plastic bags
- A pin
- Water

How to do the experiment?
1. Fill the bags with water and seal them.
2. Holding in the position shown in the picture, pierce with the pin at several places.

What will happen?
The water will flow out in different directions as the hydrostatic pressure acts on it.

Note: To help your experiment succeed, you should also pierce the water bag at the top, so that the atmospheric pressure can also act on the water.

Conclusion
Hydrostatic pressure causes the water to flow out.

Lightning from a spoon

The fact

Lightning takes place due to transfer of charge from the clouds to the Earth. Let's perform a simple experiment to observe how this transfer takes place.

What you need

- Three dry glasses
- A metal tray
- A plastic ruler
- A metal spoon
- woollen cloth

How to do the experiment?

1. Place the glasses next to each other as shown.
2. Place the tray on top of them.
3. Charge the ruler by rubbing it with the cloth and put it on top of the tray.
4. Hold the spoon close to the tray.

What will happen?

There will be an electric spark like the lightning between the tray and the spoon.

Conclusion

The electricity from the ruler flows into the tray and then jumps from it to the spoon in the form of lightning.

PHYSICS

What absorbs more heat?

The fact

When you're out in the sun on a hot summer day it is better to wear some light coloured clothes as they absorb less heat. Dark colours absorb more heat. Let us prove this through this simple experiment.

What you need

- 2 identical drinking glasses or jars
- Water
- Thermometer
- 2 elastic bands or some sellotape
- White paper
- Black paper

How to do the experiment?

1. Wrap the white paper around one of the glasses using an elastic band or sellotape to hold it on.
2. Do the same with the black paper to the other glass.
3. Fill the glasses with equal amount of water.
4. Leave the glasses out in the sun for a couple of hours before returning to measure the temperature of the water in each.

What will happen?

The glass wrapped in black paper absorbs more light and heat than the one wrapped in white paper. Measuring the temperatures of the water will show that the water in the black paper wrapped glass was hotter than the other glass. Lighter surfaces reflect more light, that's why people wear lighter coloured clothes in summer so that it keeps them cooler.

Conclusion

Dark coloured objects absorb more heat as compared to light coloured objects.

A flying ping pong ball

The fact

Gravity and air pressure play an important role. Let us show how through this simple experiment.

What you need

- At least 1 ping pong ball (2 or 3 would be great)
- A hair dryer

How to do the experiment?

1. Plug in the hair dryer and turn it on.
2. Put it on the highest setting and point it upwards.
3. Place your ping pong ball above the hair dryer and see what happens.

What will happen?

Your ping pong ball floats gently above the hair dryer without shifting sideways or flying away. The airflow from the hair dryer pushes the ping pong ball upwards until its upward force equals the force of gravity pushing down on it. When it reaches this point it gently floats where the upward and the downward forces are equal.

A step further

Try floating 2 or even 3 ping pong balls as an extra challenge.

Conclusion

Two equal and opposite forces cancel out the effect of each other.

Index

A
air resistance 4
atomizer 6

C
centre of gravity 9
charge 18, 19, 29
chromium 16
convex lens 11
convex mirror 11

E
electric battery 17
equilibrium 9
expand 25, 26

H
horizontally 4, 5, 9
hydrostatic pressure 28

I
inverted image 21

L
lightning 29

M
magnified 11
molecules 25

N
nickel 16

P
phenomenon 14
photographic film 21
pitch 12, 13, 14
pressure 5, 6, 27, 28, 31

R
radiated heat 7
resonance 14

S
sound waves 20
static charge 18
surface area 4

V
vibration 13

PEGASUS ENCYCLOPEDIA LIBRARY

Experiments and Activities
GENERAL SCIENCE

Edited by: Aparna Chatterji
Managing editor: Tapasi De
Designed by: Vijesh Chahal and Anil Kumar
Illustrated by: Suman S. Roy, Tanoy Choudhury
Colouring done by: Vinay Kumar, Sonu, Kiran Kumari & Pradeep Kumar

GENERAL SCIENCE

CONTENTS

Introduction	3
Underwater fountain	4
Erupting volcano	5
Invisible letter	6
Red cabbage, the indicator	7
Misleading depths	8
Aerodynamic paradox	9
Blowing a paper ball into a bottle	10
Water mountain	11
Water roses	12
Balancing	13
Humpty Dumpty that never falls	14
Flying apart	15
Watery merry-go-round	16
Bottle on a bottle	17
Speed of water	18
Air scales	19
How to cheat a scale	20
How to make a rainbow	21
A mini-cinema	22
Kaleidoscope	23
Misled by water	24
Water as a lens	25
A Balancing Caper	26
Push at a distance	27
Energy changes	28
Self-adhesive ice	29
The jumping coin	30
Index	32

Introduction

Learning and experiencing new things is a continuous process. Children are much more inquisitive than we elders are. They are always bubbling with enthusiasm when it comes to knowing new things. That is the reason they are so full of questions. This enthusiasm should never be curbed; instead, it should be encouraged!

It is a proven fact that children learn the most by doing, experiencing and seeing things. Teaching them through books and worksheets only, does not suffice. We all know that 'seeing is believing'.

But sometimes due to the constraint of time and many other factors, elders are not successful in giving those experiences and exposure to their children which they deserve.

Here is an encyclopedia based on General Science which is full of simple activities and experiments which the children can do by themselves. It will definitely help them to develop a rational frame of mind and also sharpen their power of reasoning.

GENERAL SCIENCE

Underwater fountain

The fact

The same liquid has different densities at different temperatures. This experiment will prove it.

What you need

- A large glass vessel filled with water
- A small glass vessel with a stopper
- Some ink

How to do the experiment?

1. Pour cold water into the large vessel.
2. Pour hot water into the small vessel, add a few drops of ink, close it and shake.
3. Place the small vessel at the bottom of the large one.
4. Remove the small vessel's stopper.

What will happen?

The warm coloured water will rise and stay on top of the cool water. After some time, the coloured and clear waters will mix.

Astonishing fact

Did you know that there is the same amount of water in the world today as when the earth was first created? The earth will not gain or lose any water because it is recycled by nature.

Conclusion

The molecules of the hot water move faster than those of the cold water. The hot water is therefore less dense and also lighter; so it tends to climb up. Once their temperatures are equalised, the coloured water will sink and mix with the clear water.

Erupting volcano

The fact

Carbon dioxide is the gas which makes carbonated drinks so fizzy. If you shake a bottle of soda and then quickly open the bottle, the gas inside bubbles and rushes out of the bottle. Carbon dioxide is also useful for other things. It is used in fire-extinguishers and also helps cakes to rise. In this experiment you will be able to form carbon dioxide bubbles.

What you need

- A small glass jar
- A saucer
- Plasticine
- Bicarbonate of soda
- Vinegar
- Red food dye
- A teaspoon

How to do the experiment?

1. Place the jar in the middle of the saucer.
2. Cover its sides with plasticine to make the shape of a volcano cone.
3. Carefully fill half the jar with bicarbonate of soda.
4. Add some red food dye to it.
5. Using the spoon, slowly pour vinegar into the soda.
6. Stand back and observe.

What will happen?

Bubbles will form in the mixture and flow over the sides of the volcano.

Conclusion

The mixture of acetic acid in the vinegar and bicarbonate of soda form bubbles of carbondioxide gas. The bubbles are light and immediately rise to the surface, and the mixture begins to foam. The foam rises and flows over the sides, just like lava in a volcano.

GENERAL SCIENCE

Invisible letter

The fact

It is possible to write a message which no one will be able to read unless you want them to. Let us see how to do this through this experiment.

What you need

- A toothpick
- Some vinegar or lemon juice
- Paper
- A candle
- Match box

How to do the experiment?

1. Break the toothpick into half and use the thicker end as a pen.
2. Dip it into vinegar or lemon juice and write a message on the paper.
3. Wait until the paper dries.
4. Light the candle and carefully hold the paper close to the flame.

What will happen?

After the message on the paper dries, it will disappear. But heating it on the flame will bring up the writing again.

What did you learn?

Once the 'ink' evaporates from the paper, the writing will not be visible. When this paper is exposed to heat, the parts which had held the 'ink' react with oxygen at a lower temperature than the rest of the paper, which makes them darker and brings up the message on the paper.

6

Red cabbage, the indicator

The fact

Red cabbage juice contains a pigment called flavin. Very acidic solutions turn flavin red in colour while basic solutions turn it green.

What you need

- Half red cabbage
- A pot of water
- A knife
- A cutting board
- Paper napkins or filter paper
- Lemon juice, vinegar and liquid soap

How to do the experiment?

1. Ask an adult to slice up the cabbage. Boil it in water for about five minutes.
2. Take the cabbage out of the water and let the water cool. Cut the paper napkins or filter paper into ribbons.
3. Dip the ribbons into the water. Let the ribbons soak.
4. Dry the ribbons. After they are dry, drip on them drops of vinegar, lemon juice and liquid soap

What will happen?

The stains on the ribbons will be of different colours.

Note: An important indicator often used by scientists is litmus.

Conclusion

Red cabbage contains a chemical which we call an indicator. Indicators change colour when you add to them acids or bases. The juice of the red cabbage turns green when it is combined with a base (for example bicarbonate of soda) and turns red again when an acid is added (for example vinegar). Instead of the cabbage you can also use the petals of sanicle, which also contain an indicator that changes colours when acids or bases are added.

GENERAL SCIENCE

Misleading depths

The fact

When light moves from one medium to another, it bends. This phenomenon is known as refraction of light. Refraction can produce strange visual effects. Let us see how.

What you need

- A glass jar
- A coin
- Water
- Cardboard

The Fact

Seas, lakes and rivers often appear less deep than they really are because refraction makes the bottom seem nearer. Fishermen, who use harpoons, never aim at the fish where their eyes see them but at a point which seems lower in water.

How to do the experiment?

1. Make a cardboard shield as shown.
2. Put the coin in the jar and put the shield in front of the jar.
3. Position yourself so you can see the top of the jar, but not the coin.
4. Tell a friend of yours to slowly pour water into the jar.

What will happen?

As water fills the jar, the coin will gradually appear on the water surface!

Conclusion

The coin has become visible due to the refraction of rays of light. On pouring water into the jar, refraction of light takes place. As a result, the coin appears to be placed at a position that is higher than its actual position. Thus, it becomes visible.

Aerodynamic paradox

The fact

Wind forces the branches of trees to bend in the direction in which it is blowing. But airstreams can also move objects in completely unexpected directions. Let us see how.

A step further

You can see the same paradox in action if you try to blow a ping-pong ball out of a funnel by blowing hard through it.

Note: we call everything that happens contrary to what can be expected a 'paradox'.

What you need

- Two pencils
- Two pieces of thin paper

How to do the experiment?

1. Hold the two pieces of paper on the pencils as shown.
2. Now blow hard between them.

What will happen?

Instead of being blown apart as you expected, the sheets will cling to each other!

Conclusion

By blowing between the two paper strips, you cause the air between the strips to move. This lessens the air pressure between the strips. On the other hand, the air pressure on the outer sides of the strips remains high which forces the strips inwards as it pushes them towards the area of lower pressure.

GENERAL SCIENCE

Blowing a paper ball into a bottle

The fact

Air pressure can move objects. Let us see how.

increases the air pressure inside the bottle. As the compressed air rushes out, it carries the paper ball out with it.

What you need

- An empty bottle
- A small paper ball

How to do the experiment?

1. Lay the bottle on the table horizontally.
2. Put the ball of paper in the neck of the bottle and try to blow it inside.

What will happen?

Instead of flying in, the ball will hit you in the face!

What did you learn?

The air that you blew into the bottle goes past the paper ball and hits the back or bottom of the bottle. This

Conclusion

Air moves from a region of high pressure to a region of low pressure.

Water mountain

The fact

It is quite amazing how many coins we can drop into a full glass of water without making it spill over the brim. Let us see how, through this experiment.

What will happen?

The water level will rise, but it will still not spill over.

What you need

- A glass of water
- Metal coins

How to do the experiment?

1. Fill the glass with water up to the very brim.
2. Put coins into the water carefully, one by one.

Conclusion

We can observe a phenomenon called surface tension. Water molecules on the surface are exposed to the action of molecular forces towards the interior of the water. They make the surface act like a stretched rubber membrane, preventing the water from spilling over.

GENERAL SCIENCE

Water roses

The fact

Absorption of water by capillaries causes them to swell and become turgid.

What you need

- Smooth paper
- A pencil
- Scissors
- A vessel with water

How to do the experiment?

1. Cut out paper flowers as shown.
2. Colour and fold the petals inwards.
3. Float the paper flowers in the vessel of water.
4. Sprinkle a few drops of water on the paper flowers.

What will happen?

The petals will open slowly.

Conclusion

Paper is made mainly of plant fibres which contain tiny tubes (capillaries). As the water enters the capillaries, the paper slowly swells and the petals slowly open.

12

Balancing

The fact

The centre of gravity is that point in an object where there is as much weight on one side as on the other. When we locate the centre of gravity in an object we can get that object to balance.

What you need

- An unopened bottle
- A cork stopper
- A needle
- Two forks

How to do the experiment?

1. Carefully stick the needle into the cork, then stick the two forks into opposite sides of the cork as shown. Balance the other end of the needle on the cap of the bottle carefully until the whole set up stands in a state of equilibrium.

A step further

Balance a ruler on a pencil held horizontally. Place various objects on the ruler's ends (erasers, sharpeners etc.). To preserve the balance, the position of the pencil will always have to be nearer the heavier of the two objects.

Conclusion

By adjusting the angle and location of the forks you can make the needle stand straight up. The needle balances because of the fact that there is exactly as much weight on one side of the needle as on the other side. The point of the needle is the centre of gravity.

Humpty Dumpty that never falls

The fact

Objects always tend to assume the most stable position possible. The lower their centre of gravity, the easier it is for them to return to a state of equilibrium. In this experiment, you can make a Humpty Dumpty who will show you this rule.

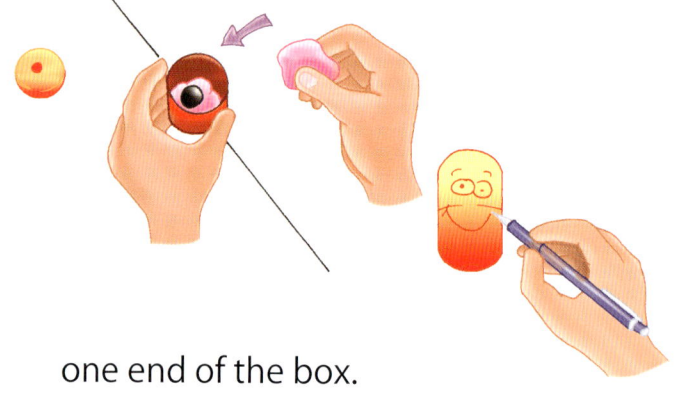

What you need

- A plastic box from the chocolate egg surprise
- A metal ball
- Plasticine
- A felt-tipped pen

How to do the experiment?

1. Fix the metal ball with the plasticine at one end of the box.
2. Close the box and draw a face on it.

What will happen?

In whichever way you move the Humpty Dumpty, it will always bounce back to the same vertical position.

Conclusion

The weight of the plasticine makes the centre of gravity of the ball occur just below the point where it touches the ground. This makes Humpty Dumpty balance and bounce back to the same vertical position.

Flying apart

The fact

Every action has an equal and opposite reaction.

What you need

- An empty matchbox
- Matches
- A razor blade
- Thread

How to do the experiment?

1. Use the thread to tie the razor blade around the box as shown.
2. Hang the box with another piece of thread as shown.
3. Break the thread holding the razor blade by burning it with a glowing matchstick.

What will happen?

The razor blade will fly to one side (action) and the box to the other (reaction).

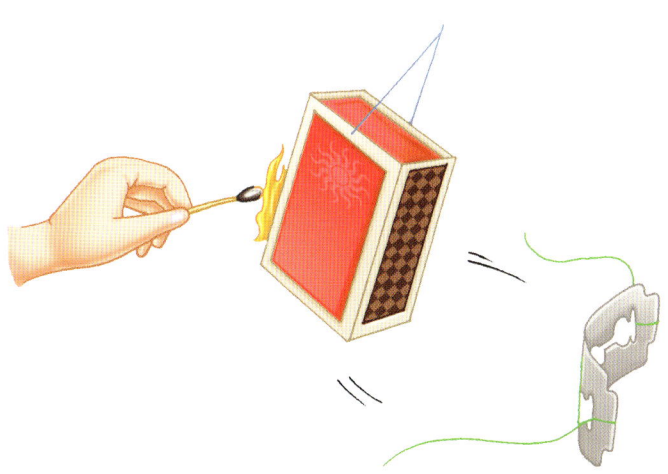

Conclusion

As the razor blade flies to one side it exerts an equal and opposite force on the box which then moves or flies off to the opposite side.

15

Watery merry-go-round

The fact

Every action has an equal and opposite reaction.

What you need

- A small plastic bottle
- Two plastic tubes
- Some string

How to do the experiment?

1. Bend the tubes, pierce the bottle and insert the tubes into the bottle. Then hang the bottle, as shown in the picture.
2. Fill the bottle with water.

What will happen?

Water will flow through the tubes and the bottle will begin to turn in a direction opposite to that of the flow of water.

Conclusion

As the water begins to flow through the tubes in a particular direction (action), the bottle begins to turn in an opposite direction (reaction).

Bottle on a bottle

The fact

Inertia tends to keep motionless objects where they are. To get things moving you have to overcome inertia of rest. In other words, "A body at rest tends to remain at rest."

What you need

- Two bottles of glass
- A piece of thin cardboard

How to do the experiment?

1. Place the bottles on top of each other with the cardboard between them as shown.
2. Pull away the cardboard sharply.

What will happen?

The upper bottle will retain its state of rest.

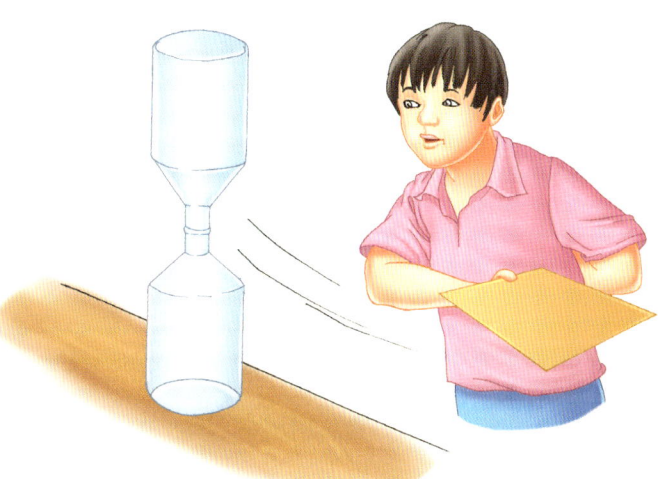

Warning!

Quite a lot of skill is needed for performing this trick. You can practice for it by surrounding the bottom bottle with pillows so the top one doesn't break if it falls.

Conclusion

The bottle on the top remains standing still as inertia tends to keep it that way. The card snaps away so quickly that the bottle on the top has no chance to follow the card. Gravity pulls it down on the bottle at the bottom.

17

GENERAL SCIENCE

Speed of water

The fact

We know what speed is from our everyday life. If objects traverse different paths in the same period of time, we say that their speeds differ. How can we determine the speed at which water flows in a river?

What you need

- Two wooden pegs
- A piece of wood
- A stopwatch or watch having a second hand

How to do the experiment?

1. Fix the pegs on the river bank. They will be your objects of reference.
2. Measure the distance between the pegs.
3. Throw the piece of wood into the river and see how long it takes it to pass from one peg to the other.
4. Divide the distance by the time elapsed. You will get a figure showing the speed, to which, add the unit of measurement (metres per second or m/s).

A step further

You can measure the speed of an electric train in the same manner, if you know the distance between the poles carrying the wire feed.

Conclusion

Speed is defined as the distance covered by an object per unit time. Mathematically, speed=Distance/Time

Air scales

The fact

We know that hot air is lighter than cold air.

What you need

- An old ruler
- Two plastic cups
- Three pieces of string
- A candle
- Matches
- Scissors
- A drill

How to do the experiment?

1. Drill three holes on the ruler, one in the middle and the others near the ends at an equal distance from the middle.
2. Suspend the cups at the ends as shown in the picture.
3. Suspend the whole set up as shown and balance it.
4. Light the candle and place it under the cup suspended upside-down

What will happen?

The side of the ruler with the candle will go upwards.

Conclusion

As it is heated by the candle, the air in the cup expands and becomes lighter, upsetting the whole balance.

GENERAL SCIENCE

How to cheat a scale

The fact

Weight of an object on Earth is the force with which the Earth pulls it towards itself due to gravity.

What you need

- A household weighing machine

How to do the experiment?

1. Stand on the machine as you usually do.
2. Stretch out your hands before you and bend your knees quickly.
3. As you stand on the machine, raise your hands rapidly.
4. Watch what the scale indicates in both cases.

What will happen?

When you bend your knees the scale shows a smaller weight and when you raise your hands a greater one.

Conclusion

As you squat, for a moment your body is in a state of freefall, in which it has no weight. As a result, the scale shows a decreased weight. As you lift your hands, they 'rest' on the body a little more, and a slight increase in weight can be seen.

How to make a rainbow

The fact

We always marvel at a rainbow's colours, we usually see after a shower of rain. But it is possible to make a rainbow even without rain! Let us see how.

What you need

- A glass
- A piece of cardboard with a very thin (1 millimetre) slit
- White paper
- Water

How to do the experiment?

1. Fill the glass with water and place it on the paper.
2. Lean the cardboard against the glass with the slit in a vertical position.
3. Turn the two towards the sun.

What will happen?

A rainbow will be seen on the paper.

Conclusion

The water acts as a prism which breaks down the sun's light into the colours of the rainbow.

21

GENERAL SCIENCE

A mini-cinema

The fact

The human eye tends to retain the image of an object for a short time even after the object has been removed. The image persists for about one sixteenth of a second. Hence, if more than 16 images are flashed within one second, the human eye fuses one image into the other and the impression of movement is formed. Let us see how.

What you need

- Cardboard
- Paper strips with drawings showing a moving object
- Scissors

How to do the experiment?

1. Make two parallel slits on the cardboard. Make sure the distance between the slits equals the size of the drawings.
2. Now pass the strip of picture through the slits as shown in the picture.
3. Pull the strip through the slits quickly.

What will happen?

The figures in the drawing will appear to be moving!

Conclusion

The illusion is formed by the slowness of the human eye, which retains an image for a short time after it disappears. The successive images fuse into one another and an impression of movement is formed.

Kaleidoscope

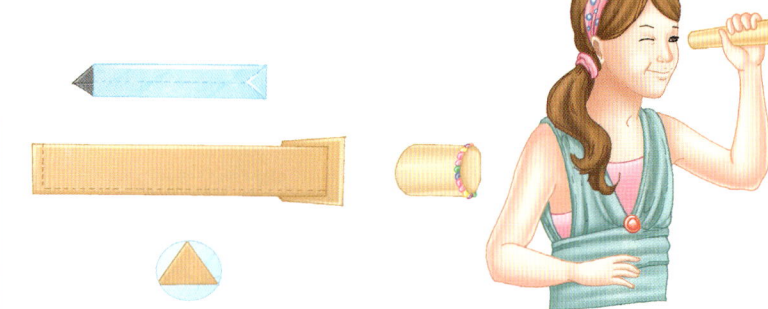

The fact

Plane mirrors are used for many devices, one of which is a toy—a kaleidoscope, which is an interesting device which will give you hours of fun. Its popular name is a children's cinema. Let's see how to make one.

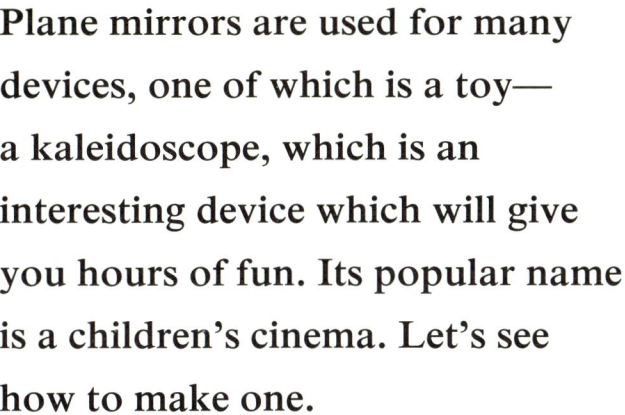

What you need

- A cardboard tube
- Cardboard
- Three long and identical pieces of mirror or plane glass
- Small bits of glass in different colours
- Thick transparent PVC foil or cellophane
- Adhesive tape
- Scissors

How to do the experiment?

1. Tape the mirror (glass) pieces so as to make a three-sided prism (1).
2. Make a circular cardboard cover (2) and tape it to one end of the prism.
3. Insert the prism into the tube.
4. Tape the transparent foil on to the other end of the tube (4)
5. Make a shorter cardboard tube slightly wider than the first one and then also tape foil over it (5).
6. Place a dozen pieces of glass into the second tube, slide it over the narrower tube and seal with tape so the glass pieces are free to move around.
7. Point the kaleidoscope towards a light source, look through the viewing hole (2), and slowly rotate the Kaleidoscope.

What will happen?

You will see beautiful patterns that will change constantly as you turn the kaleidoscope.

Conclusion

The glass pieces are reflected many times in the three mirrors, forming symmetrical patterns.

GENERAL SCIENCE

Misled by water

The fact

When light enters from one medium to another, it bends and changes its way. This is known as refraction. Let us see how.

What you need

- Two large glass tumblers
- One smaller glass
- Three spoons
- Water

How to do the experiment?

1. Fill the glasses with water.
2. Position them as shown in the picture.
3. Place a spoon in each as shown.

What will happen?

The spoon handles can be seen in their normal positions, but those parts seen through the water look magnified and broken, while you can see two spoons in the smaller glass! It looks as if one spoon has been moved from the bigger glass into the smaller one!

Conclusion

The refraction of light makes the spoons look broken. The water in the glass acts as a lens and makes those parts of the spoons which are inside it look bigger. Since the surface of separation, which in this case is the glass tumbler, is curved, the refraction of light makes the spoons look bigger than they actually are.

Refraction can also make an object appear to be in a different position to what it really is. In this case, refraction causes the image of the spoon in the left-hand-side large glass to be formed in the smaller glass.

24

Water as a lens

The fact

When rays of light pass from water to air, they change direction. In other words, the rays get refracted. Refraction across a curved surface leads to the formation of an enlarged image.

What will happen?

The image of the house when viewed through the jar will appear bigger, as if you are looking at it through a magnifying glass.

What you need

- A drawing of a house
- A transparent glass jar
- Water

How to do the experiment?

1. Tell someone to hold the drawing upright behind the jar which you have filled with water.
2. Move the drawing until the image appears sharp.
3. Look at the image of the house through the jar directly.

Conclusion

Due to its spherical shape, the water in the jar acts as a convex lens and forms a magnified image of the house.

GENERAL SCIENCE

A Balancing Caper

The fact

If you want to keep your body in a state of balance, its centre of gravity and your contact with the ground must be on the same vertical line. This rule can be tested in the following ways.

How to do the experiment?

1. Stand up straight with your back against a wall. Without bending your knees, try to pick up a pencil from the floor. Can you do it?

2. Sit on a chair with your back straight and your legs bent at the knees at right angles. Now try to get up without leaning forward or without tucking your feet under the chair. Can you do it? No matter how much you try, you will not be able to do it.

What will happen?

Here is why you are not able to perform the desired movements. As you sit in the chair, the vertical line passing through your centre of gravity passes through the floor somewhere between the chair legs. When you try to get up, the support is shifted to your feet and your centre of gravity isn't above them, so you lose your balance and fall back in the chair. This explanation is applicable to the first situation also.

Conclusion

When you bend over, your balancing point moves forward. To keep your balance you have to move your feet forward too. The balancing point of an object is called its centre of gravity.

Push at a distance

The fact

Like poles of magnets repel each other whereas opposite poles attract. Let us see how.

What you need

- Two bar magnets with opposite poles
- A toy lorry
- A sticky tape

How to do the experiment?

1. Fix the bar magnet on the lorry with the help of the sticky tape.
2. Use the other magnet to draw the lorry towards it, as shown in the picture.

What will happen?

When you bring the same poles closer, you push the lorry away. When you bring the opposite pole closer to the lorry, you pull it towards yourself.

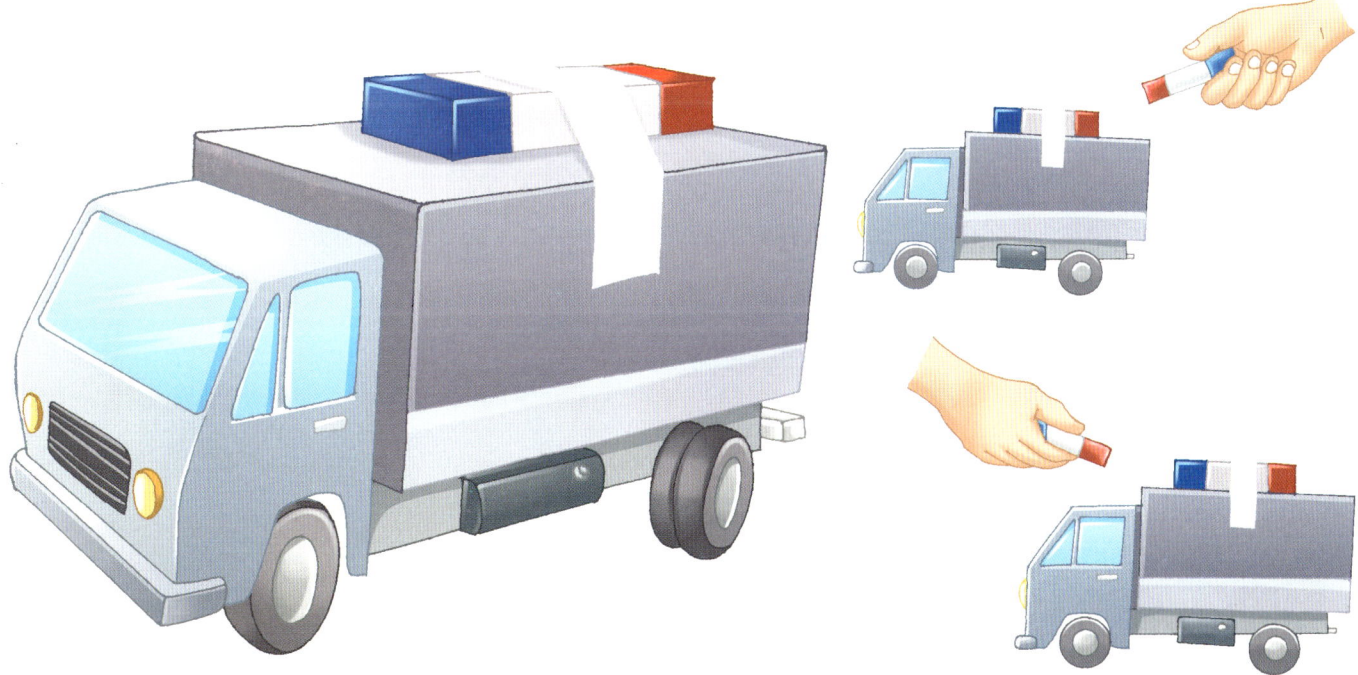

Conclusion

The movement of the lorry is determined by the magnetic force. Opposite poles of the magnets attract each other and hence the magnets are pulled closer while like or similar poles repel each other and are pushed apart.

GENERAL SCIENCE

Energy changes

The fact

Energy can neither be created nor destroyed during the course of a physical or a chemical change. It can only be transformed from one form to another.

What you need

- A broad rubber band.

How to do the experiment?

1. Stretch the band between two fingers.
2. Touch your forehead with the band.
3. Now stretch it out and quickly touch your forehead with it.

What will happen?

The second time around the band will feel warmer.

Conclusion

When you stretch out the band you move its molecules further apart, whereby they gain so-called elastic potential energy. As you release the tension, the molecules return to their original positions, but the energy used is not lost; it is transformed into heat energy. This experiment proves the validity of the rule that energy can neither be created nor destroyed.

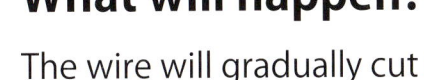

Self-adhesive ice

The fact

It is possible to melt ice even without applying heat; pressure can also melt ice.

What you need

- A bottle with a wide neck
- A piece of ice
- Thin metal wire
- Two weights (heavy objects)

How to do the experiment?

1. Place the ice on top of the bottle.
2. Put the wire across the ice and tie the weights to the ends of the wire.

What will happen?

The wire will gradually cut its way through the ice.

A step further

Place two flat pieces of ice on top of each other with a piece of wood and a heavy object on top. Two or three minutes later take off the wood and the weight and try to separate the two pieces of ice. It will not be easy! The reason is the same as in the former experiment.

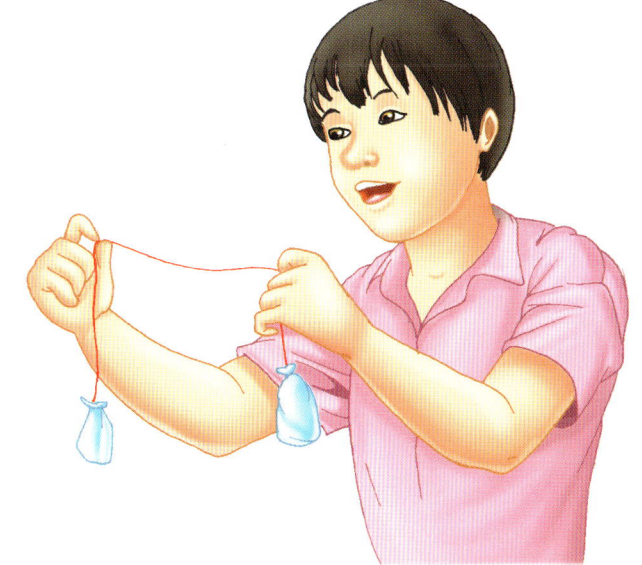

Conclusion

The pressure exerted by the wire on the ice causes friction and an increase in the wire's temperature. The warmed wire then melts the ice and passes through it. The water formed by this process re-freezes very soon and the piece of ice looks completely intact!

GENERAL SCIENCE

The jumping coin

The fact

Air and other gases expand easily when heated. How can we show the expansion of air?

What you need

- An empty glass
- Bottle with a flat top
- A metal coin

How to do the experiment?

1. Moisten the coin with water.
2. Place it on top of the bottle so that air cannot pass by it.
3. Hold the bottle in your hands for a short period of time. Ensure that your palms cover the bottle completely.

What will happen?

The coin will begin to rise and fall, as if it was jumping.

Conclusion

The warmth of your hands is transferred to the bottle as heat, and from the bottle also to the air in it. The air expands, and exerts pressure and therefore also a force on the coin. The experiment is even easier to perform if you immerse the bottle into hot water or hold it over a hot cooker plate.

A step further

Experiment 1

Take two bottles and close their mouths with rubber membranes with some string. Put one of the bottles next to a source of heat (a radiator, the kitchen cooker) and the other into the refrigerator. On the first bottle the membrane will soon bulge out (air expands when it is heated), and on the second it will be sucked into the bottle as the air has been cooled and has contracted.

Experiment 2

Take a pane of glass and raise one side of it on some support. Moisten the edge of a tumbler well and put it on the pane upside-down.

Put a burning candle close to the edge of the tumbler. Soon the tumbler will slip away from the flame. The air in the tumbler will expand and try to escape, but wont be able to do so on account of the water between the tumbler and the pane of glass. The pressure of the heated air will move the tumbler, which will slip, as the layer of water between the tumbler and the glass reduces the friction.

Did you know?

Soil is a mixture of dead plants, animals and tiny pieces of broken rocks. Soils maybe sandy, chalky or clayey.

Index

A
absorption 12
aerodynamic paradox 9

B
bases 7
bicarbonate of soda 5, 7

C
capillaries 12
centre of gravity 13, 14, 26
chemical change 28

E
equilibrium 13, 14

F
fire-extinguishers 5
flavin 7
friction 29, 31

I
inertia 17

K
kaleidoscope 23

L
litmus 7

M
magnified 24, 25
magnifying glass 25
measurement 18
molecules 4, 11, 28

P
prism 21, 23

R
refraction 8, 24, 25

S
spherical 25
surface tension 11
symmetrical 23

T
temperatures 4